CONTAINER GARDENING

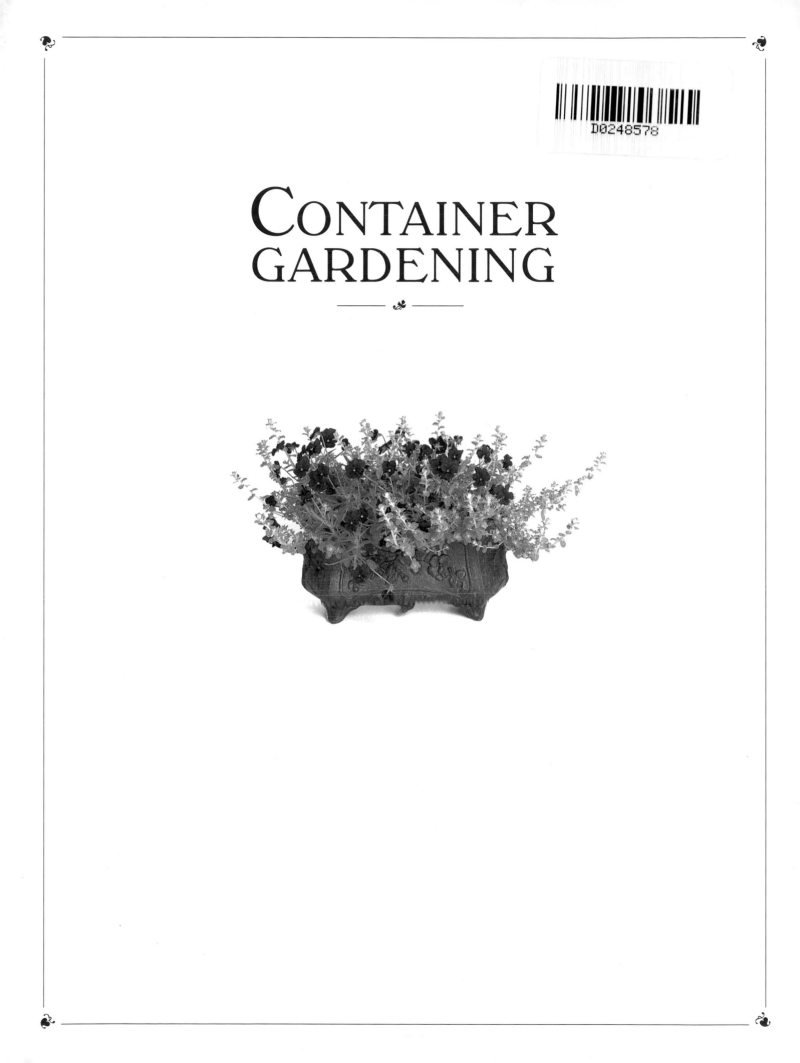

CONTAINER GARDENING

❧

MALCOLM HILLIER

Photography by

MATTHEW WARD

DORLING KINDERSLEY
London • New York • Stuttgart

A DORLING KINDERSLEY BOOK

PROJECT EDITOR
Mary-Clare Jerram

ART EDITOR
Kevin Ryan

EDITOR
Susan Thompson

MANAGING EDITOR
Jane Laing

SENIOR ART EDITOR
David Robinson

PRODUCTION MANAGER
Maryann Rogers

First published in
Great Britain in 1991
by Dorling Kindersley Limited,
9 Henrietta Street,
London WC2E 8PS
Reprinted 1991 (twice)
1992 (three times)
1993 (twice)
1994

Copyright © 1991
Dorling Kindersley, London
Text copyright © 1991
Malcolm Hillier

A CIP catalogue record for this
book is available from the
British Library

ISBN 0-86318-604-1

Computer page make-up by
The Cooling Brown Partnership
in Great Britain
Reproduced by Columbia
in Singapore
Printed and bound by
Butler and Tanner in Great Britain

CONTENTS

6 INTRODUCTION

12 PLANTING
SCHEMES

14 WINDOW BOXES
16 PERFUME AND PETUNIAS
18 SUN LOVERS FOR A WINDOW SILL
20 SHIMMERING FLOWERS AND FOLIAGE
22 THE LAST OF SUMMER
24 HAZE OF HEATHERS
26 ARRAY OF EVERGREENS
28 TERRACOTTA BAROQUE
30 FAVOURED HELLEBORES

32 POTS
34 JUST TULIPS
36 TOWERS FOR FLOWERS
38 ELEGANT COMPANIONS
40 FLAMBOYANT AZALEAS
42 SPRING NARCISSI
43 ROSES ALL SUMMER

44 PINK PELARGONIUMS
46 TENDER, FLOWERING SHRUBS
48 VARIEGATED PELARGONIUMS
50 LILIES AND BELLFLOWERS
51 PALACE PURPLE
52 CASCADING DIASCIAS
53 STRIKING-LEAVED BEGONIAS
54 SUMMER SHADE LOVERS
56 QUARTET OF GLAZED POTS
58 DECORATIVE BERRIES
59 CHRYSANTHEMUM TREE

60 LOW BOWLS
62 FLOWERING BERGENIAS
63 SPRING BLUES
64 CHINESE BOWL OF SUN ROSES
66 PINK AND MAUVE TRIO

68 URNS AND JARS
70 FOUNTAIN OF FLOWERS
71 CHINESE JAR
72 STATELY SPLENDOUR

74 BARRELS AND TUBS
76 BLUE CONIFER
78 VINE BARREL
80 BARREL OF PETUNIAS
82 CROCK OF ROSES
83 SUMMER SALAD

84 SINKS AND TROUGHS
86 WOODLAND GARDEN
88 MARINE THEME
90 WOODEN TROUGH OF EVERGREENS

92 HANGING BASKETS
94 TRADITIONAL BASKET
96 GOLD SUMMER BASKET
97 BASKET OF RED AND SILVER
98 HAYRACK OF FLOWERS
100 CLASHING-COLOURED ANNUALS
101 SPRING COLLECTION
102 MOSS BASKETS

104 SUITING THE SITE

106 SUNNY POSITIONS
108 FLOWER-FILLED PERGOLA
110 SCHEMES FOR SUN
112 PLANTS FOR SUN

114 SEMI-SHADY POSITIONS
116 CITY COURTYARD
118 SCHEMES FOR SEMI-SHADE
120 PLANTS FOR SEMI-SHADE

122 SHADY POSITIONS
124 SHADY RETREAT
126 SCHEMES FOR SHADE
128 PLANTS FOR SHADE

130 EXPOSED POSITIONS
132 ROOF TOP OF TREES
134 SCHEMES FOR EXPOSED POSITIONS
136 PLANTS FOR EXPOSED SITES

138 SPECIFIC LOCATIONS
140 PERGOLAS AND ARBOURS
142 FLIGHTS OF STEPS
144 DOORWAYS
146 WALLS AND FENCES
148 GARDEN PATHS
150 EVENING GARDEN

152 MAKING AND DECORATING CONTAINERS

154 PLANTING A BASKET
156 CONVERTING A CHIMNEY POT
158 DISGUISING A SINK
160 USING AN OLD MOP BUCKET

162 MAKING A WOODEN WINDOW BOX
164 DECORATING WOODEN WINDOW BOXES
166 EVERGREEN TOPIARY
168 CONSTRUCTING A HERB TOWER
170 TRAINING STANDARDS
172 SUPPORTING PLANTS IN POTS

174 PLANT CARE

176 PESTS AND DISEASES
178 PLANTING AND REPOTTING
180 WATERING
181 PRUNING AND DEADHEADING
182 PROPAGATION

184 PLANT LISTS
188 INDEX
192 ACKNOWLEDGMENTS

INTRODUCTION

Plants have been grown in decorative and utilitarian containers for thousands of years. From early mosaics and writings, we know that the ancient Egyptians, Greeks, and Romans grew aromatic plants, such as myrtle, box, and bay, in clay pots. They were aware that it was a practical and efficient growing technique, especially in areas where the soil was poor or shallow.

In southern Spain, during the early part of the second millennium, the Moors created wonderfully decorative, enclosed, and intimate gardens using many containers. Two famous gardens laid out in the middle of the fourteenth century, at the Alhambra and the Generalife in Granada, survive to this day. They have now been restored and, although they are not completely accurate reproductions of the originals, they still contain the essence of their early design and planting.

MEDIEVAL GARDENS

In Britain, early illustrated manuscripts of the twelfth, thirteenth, and fourteenth centuries show pots of plants growing in palaces and monastic gardens. However, it was not until the fifteenth and sixteenth centuries that there was a great blossoming of creative gardening. Inspired by the Italians, these designs frequently featured planted containers, often made from stone and lead. In northern Europe, tub-grown citrus fruit trees, emulating the plantings of the Mediterranean countries, were wheeled outside from the shelter of their orangeries during the warmer summer weather to decorate formal, paved terraces.

THE LAST TWO CENTURIES

The same inspiration fired the Victorians with enthusiasm. Production of all types of containers, small as well as large, proliferated during the nineteenth century. They manufactured copies of classical urns in cast iron, as well as the traditional materials: stone, lead, and terracotta. They made elaborate, garlanded and swagged pots for standing on terraces beside well-manicured lawns, and in summer planted them with tender exotics that had been brought on in the greenhouse.

The Edwardians, too, cherished a great love of gardens. Conservatories were all the rage, and they moved pots of begonias, bellflowers, fuchsias, plumbagos, and schizanthus from the conservatory, into the house and garden to provide extra colour and emphasis.

Nowadays, containers are widely used in almost every garden you see. Even people without a garden can have a window box or hanging basket on an outside wall. Pots and tubs are invaluable in gardens where growing space is at a premium, but they are also useful for decorating paved terraces, roof gardens, and balconies.

PANSY BASKET
A small, rustic basket of pansies, planted to make a simple feature in a Victorian garden in England. It might have been displayed on a table or bench.

MOORISH INFLUENCE
Decorative containers of plants were used extensively at the fourteenth-century Alhambra gardens, established by the Moors in Granada, Spain.

CORRECT CONDITIONS

Growing plants is one of life's greatest pleasures. It is so simple, either to start them off from seed or to buy them once they are over their teething problems and tantrums, and raise them, watching the response to a little loving care. I cannot pretend that all plants are easy to grow, but the great majority ask for little more than to be planted in the correct potting mixture, to be given enough water – as well as a little nourishment – from time to time, and to be placed in the right situation. They are rarely over fussy and soon adapt to conditions which, while they may not be absolutely ideal, are not diametrically opposed to their likes and dislikes. These requirements are factors that I will look at in the following chapters, so that you can assess which plants you may like to grow together and where, in the places available, they will give you their very best display.

Growing in containers is a very controlled method of raising plants. Each plant, or group of plants, can be given exactly the right type of soil and amounts of water and food. The situation chosen for the placing of the container must be taken into account when selecting the plants. Sun or shade, exposed or sheltered, very cold or more temperate, are all factors that can make or break a display in a very short period. The majority of plants like to grow and flower in sunny or partially sunny positions. A smaller number enjoy the shade, and only a few plants are happy in very exposed places.

The elements are harsher on plants in containers, than on their counterparts grown in richly cultivated garden beds or borders. Heat and winds dry out pots and plants in containers quickly, rain does not easily reach their limited soil area, and extreme cold can freeze the pot and root ball solid. However, you can control the watering, and make sure that you place plants that are adversely affected by winds in sheltered positions. If you live in a cold area, avoid growing the more tender plants, or if you are determined to, take measures to protect them from frost. You can wrap vulnerable specimens in sacking or a good layer of bracken and, if space permits, sink the container into the ground for the winter. The best solution, particularly for plants like marguerites and standard fuchsias, is to take them into a greenhouse, conservatory, or a garden shed which has some windows.

A DESERVING SITE

Container plantings have the benefit of being raised above ground level which gives them greater importance and visual impact, but you should still make sure the plants are being seen and enjoyed to their best advantage, without making them inaccessible for the day-to-day maintenance. One of the most enjoyable summer pastimes is eating outside, so grow pots of sweetly scented plants close to the garden table: lavender, tobacco plants, lilies, night-scented

NATURAL STONE CONTAINER
The crevices in a wall can be treated like a container garden, and planted with species that require only a little soil. Here, aubrieta and grape hyacinths grow.

stock, aromatic-leaved pelargoniums, or climbers such as trachelospermum, datura, summer-flowering jasmine, or honeysuckle.

✗ Always consider the ultimate size of the plant in relation to its chosen site. If windows are small, for example, it is inadvisable to grow large plants in a window box, as they will block the light from the room. Conversely, if you place a planting in front of a fence or wall, select something that will grow tall and wide against it. Anything too small will be lost against a large expanse.

TYPES OF CONTAINERS

The size of container needs careful consideration. It must neither swamp the plant, nor make it top heavy and put it at the mercy of the winds. And it must be large enough to allow room for proper root development, especially if you intend to grow the larger shrubs and trees.

✗ Containers that have a natural affinity to their surroundings are usually the most attractive. Clay, wood, and stone are my first choices, followed by the materials that simulate them: reconstituted stone, fibreglass, and good plastic. Choose pots that relate to nearby architectural details. Containers in terracotta, natural wood, and stone look good against traditional building materials, while simulated reconstituted stone, white or coloured plastic, and fibreglass suit the more austere situations where the background is glass or painted walling, or the paving is a new material.

✗ In addition to the less usual containers, such as strawberry pots and herb pots, improvised containers can be most effective. Old chimney pots, galvanized buckets, and large, painted tins, crates, stone and ceramic sinks, fish kettles, bread crocks, old saucepans, large shells, a wheelbarrow, metal or plastic bins, or hollowed-out tree trunks can all be used to great effect, at minimal cost.

✗ Containers always work well grouped together. Plant large shrubs or trees in the big containers placed at the back of the collection, and perhaps fill the lower containers in front with annuals, bulbs, and low-growing perennials. There are no rules about grouping containers, although I find that it is generally better not to have too many different types of container in the same area.

WEATHERING EFFECTS

Most containers look better when they are well weathered. Left in the sun, patches of white will appear on terracotta, as the salts in the clay leach

STONE AND TERRACOTTA
A weathered pot on a terrace bursts with hosta leaves, the silver foliage of a helichrysum, and the flowers of chrysanthemum, verbena, and pelargoniums. Notice how the terracotta blends with the stone slabs.

out. In shade, moss and lichen will start to grow on the sides of the pot and its colour will change, sometimes deepening to a dark rust and sometimes lightening to peach and sandy hues. You can speed up the aging process by painting live yoghurt, soot, and manure on to porous containers; make sure that you coat their top rim as well as their sides.

TEMPORARY OR PERMANENT

Some container plantings are relatively permanent; the plants can stay in the same pot for many years. Other arrangements can be more temporary, perhaps planted to look attractive for just one or two seasons. As temporary plantings pass their best, provided they are not too heavy, you can move them to less prominent situations. Alternatively, dismantle them and replace the plants with others for the future. A third alternative is to add seasonal colour to the more permanent plantings, if there is sufficient space in the container.

SPRING COLOUR
Scarlet tulips (LEFT) grow in an ancient copper pot, corroded by the weather to a stunning, rich, bluey green hue. When the flowers have finished, transplant the bulbs to a border in the garden, and fill the container with colourful bedding annuals for a display during the summer months and into the early autumn.

LEAFY FOIL
A rich planting of fuchsias, geraniums, and lobelias, crammed into an old wooden cart (BELOW). Evergreens, such as the ivy and golden euonymus seen here, are invaluable, providing a leafy foil to the more seasonal flowering annuals.

Permanent plantings can consist of shrubs, trees, or perennials, either grown as single specimens, or as a grouping of several of the same type of plant in one container. Temporary, seasonal plantings consist of annuals, biennials, and bulbs that look attractive in mixed selections, as well as planted on their own. Before container-grown shrubs or trees have grown too large, and produced root sytems that take up most of the container, they can be underplanted with seasonal colour or more permanent trailing plants.

Most annuals grow better in the right container than in the open ground, whereas containerised shrubs, trees, and climbers, although they will grow well, tend not to reach the same size that they would if planted in open ground.

FLOWERS, FOLIAGE, AND FRAGRANCE

The flowering capabilities of shrubs and perennials grown in containers are not as great as for those grown in the open, and so it is wise to consider the benefits of the foliage as well as flowers. If the position receives sun or half-sun, you can consider a host of wonderful plants with attractive leaves, ranging in colour from normal green through gold, lime, and yellow, to grey, silver, and white, and rust, copper, pink, purple, and plum. The choice for a shady place is slightly more limited, but there are still interesting combinations of plant form, leaf shape or texture, and flowers.

Fragrance is an essential part of the garden. Until quite recently the perfume of flowers, which was so valued in the seventeenth, eighteenth, and nineteenth centuries, had been rather neglected. During this century, the emphasis has been on breeding flowers just for their shape, size, and colour; scent has not been a major consideration. Now, perfume is again becoming important, with plant catalogues describing the fragrances of new garden hybrids in glowing terms. Great steps have been made in

FLOWERS EVERY SUMMER
The African lilies in the wooden tubs lining this sunny, wooden deck will flower year after year, provided the winter is not too cold. They thrive when grown in containers as their roots favour cramped conditions.

developing new roses that have all the characteristics of the old roses: flower shape, colour, and perfume. To these characteristics, the advantage of a long flowering season has now been added. Plenty of the smaller-growing roses – the varieties most suitable for container culture – have delicious, rich scents.

SEASONAL CHANGES

Summer is the time for the most colourful and sumptuous displays, and this is also when we can enjoy them outside for their form, colour combinations, and scent. The most popular summer plants have not won their place by chance. They are the ones, like pelargoniums, that give a splendid show of flowers over a long period. Many summer plantings continue through the autumn, especially if the weather is neither too cold nor windy. Chrysanthemums and asters are the epitome of autumn with their rich pinks, reds, and oranges and give a vibrant display.

Rich, winter evergreens can give endless pleasure, enhancing the external views from the warm safety of your house during the cold and often grey months. Spring too, can be brought close to the windows, with bulbs and other early-flowering plants, either in window boxes or in pots near the house. Our aim should always be to stimulate the senses as much as possible. Container gardening provides you with the chance to create plantings of all shapes and sizes, using trees, shrubs, annuals, perennials, and bulbs, all of which are glorious for their combinations of flower, leaf, and fragrance.

PLANTING SCHEMES

❧

COMBINING PLANTS THAT ENJOY each other's company, and growing them in containers, gives great pleasure. The colour of flowers and leaves, their shapes and perfumes, are exciting elements with which to play. Pale or bright, tamed or wild, let the plants be an inspiration for your container arrangements.

HOT SUMMER
Cascading pelargoniums, bedding dahlias, and malvastrum make a vibrant summer planting.

WINDOW BOXES

ON A COLD winter's morning, I love looking out of the kitchen window at the rich, golden-green plants sitting in the window boxes, just beyond the pane of glass. It is a spot that never catches the sun, but it is quite bright and the plants always look happy. Nearly everyone can have a window box or two, even if they live high above the ground with no garden at the front or back. Of course, window boxes need not be used only in window recesses. They can look most effective resting on the ground against a wall or a fence, or edging a balcony so that trailing plants can cascade down the side of the building.

CLOSE FIT

Window boxes on sills look best if they almost fit the window recess. Boxes are manufactured in a range of sizes, so that it is usually possible to find one that is a suitable size for your sill. They are also made in a great range of materials: plastic, fibreglass, composition wood, and terracotta. Some of the plastic ones are not very strong. In the middle, they tend to bulge outwards with the weight of soil, although clips are available from stores to help keep the box in shape. They are the cheapest, and they are mostly available in white, black, and green. Stronger plastic window boxes are sold in various forms, but I find that the plainer ones look best. Fibreglass is a more expensive material, but it is rigid and will last for many years. Plain designs and models made to resemble lead or painted wood are available.

✄ Wooden boxes always look good because of their natural affinity to plant material, but they will eventually rot, even if well-treated with wood preservatives and painted every year. You

INFORMAL IVY SETTING
A small terracotta box (ABOVE) decorated with angels' heads, and filled with pinks, swan river daisies, and verbena sits comfortably on the ledge of an ivy-covered wall.

FRENCH-STYLE WINDOW BOX
A mass of ivy-leaved pelargoniums (LEFT), tumble out of a window box in France. To achieve this effect, the pelargoniums should be planted 18-20cm (7-8in) apart.

can get around this problem by using a well-made plastic box that fits your sill, with a little room to spare at each side, and then making a wooden cover for it. You drop the newly planted plastic box into the completed, wooden cover. When choosing a colour for your wooden cover, it is best to let the plants be the masters of the box: extremely brightly coloured or over-decorated boxes can detract from the natural beauty of the flowers and foliage in your planting.

TERRACOTTA OPTION

Because of the beautiful, natural, quality of terracotta, I find that window boxes made in this material always tend to look most effective. Before buying anything, measure up your window sill to ensure a good fit. Bear in mind that in exposed situations soft terracotta can easily flake and crack, so in cold areas it may be best to avoid using it, except during the warm summer and early autumn months, before the frosts arrive.

SAFE AND SECURE

Window boxes can be extremely heavy, especially when they have been watered, so you must fix them securely in place. On sills that slope gently forwards, chock up the front of the box, slightly, to keep it level, and secure metal brackets either to the sides of the window recess or on the sill itself, to prevent the window box from slipping forwards.

✄ Window box arrangements in sunny spots need plenty of water in hot summer weather, so prevent excess water running down the sides of the building by placing a tray under the box. Plastic trays are available from most garden centres. Remember not to leave the container sitting in water.

PERFUME AND PETUNIAS

IT IS ALL TOO EASY to plant the same old favourite annuals every year, knowing that they will do well, flower for three or even four months a year, and provide plenty of colour. For greater interest, I try to use my favourites in combination with some lesser-known plants.

Here, petunias – immensely hard-working plants producing masses of flowers in summer – are associated with the sweetly scented, rich purple heads of heliotrope, spikes of cream and purple salvias, and variegated pink and silver-leaved trails of wandering Jew – plants that all thrive when grown together. Remember that petunias should be planted in new soil each season to ensure that they will not suffer from petunia wilt passed on from the previous year. Otherwise they need little attention, except for watering and a weekly feed of liquid fertilizer.

PRACTICAL MATTERS

SOIL
Plant in a well-drained potting mixture of medium nutritional value.

SITE
Place in a sunny position.

WATERING
Keep well-watered but not soggy. Give a liquid feed once a week.

PLANTS
Grow four petunias, three heliotrope, three salvias, and three wandering Jews in a 75cm- (30in-) long, terracotta window box.

✎ PLANTING UP A WINDOW BOX ✎

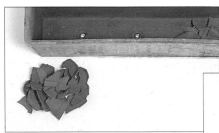

1 *Thoroughly clean the window box with warm water and a mild detergent. Lightly cover the drainage holes at the base with clean crocks.*

2 *Half fill the window box with a well-drained potting mixture of medium nutritional value. If the potting mixture has dried out, damp it down with water before you start to plant up.*

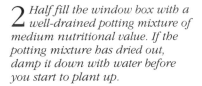

3 *Experiment with the positioning of the plants while they are still in their pots until you are happy with the effect, placing the taller plants at the rear, and the trailing ones at the sides and towards the front. Turn the plants out of their pots, loosen the roots at the base of each root ball, then firm the plants into place with more potting mixture. When the planting is completed, the soil level should be about 2cm (¾in) below the top of the planter, to facilitate watering.*

Plant Positions

✗ The heliotrope (RIGHT) tends to become straggly, so it is best planted at the back of the window box. Initially, pinch out the growing tips to encourage bushy growth. Position the petunias and wandering Jew towards the front, with the upright salvias between. Plant in early summer. This arrangement will flower for only one season.

Heliotrope
(Heliotropium peruvianum)
The scent of the flowers is reminiscent of cooked cherries, hence its common name of 'cherry pie'.

Petunia *(Petunia x hybrida* Star Series)
The white-striped flowers come in a wide range of cheerful colours.

Salvia *(Salvia splendens* Cleopatra Series)
Spikes of flowers appear throughout the summer and early autumn.

Victorian Theme

✗ The rich plum, purple, and white colouring of the petunias, heliotrope, salvias, and trailing, wandering Jew, growing in an old window box gives the arrangement a slight Victorian feel.

Wandering Jew *(Tradescantia fluminensis* 'Variegata')
A good trailing plant for a window box of summer annuals.

SUN LOVERS FOR A WINDOW SILL

I LIKE PLANTINGS that make a positive statement. This does not necessarily mean that the colours should always be brilliant, nor that the leaf and flower shapes of the various species should be strikingly different. It suggests that the arrangement should have a sense of structure about it, which makes it look both inevitable and interesting.

In this summer window box, yellow gazanias spill down over the edge of the container, below mounds of delicate foliage and large gold and cream zinnia flowers, leaving the sides exposed in an unexpected way. Notice how well all the colours work together: although the scheme is predominantly gold and yellow, silver gazania leaves and white and yellow, golden feverfew flowers were introduced for contrast. I do not believe in adhering to rules relating to colour and form because, if you do, the plantings tend to become boring and predictable. Give free rein to your imagination. Successful arrangements combine common sense with a touch of daring.

Zinnia (*Zinnia elegans*)
For optimum flowering, deadhead regularly.

Golden marjoram (*Origanum vulgare* 'Aureum')
A delicious herb that looks good, too.

Golden feverfew (*Chrysanthemum parthenium* 'Aureum')
Cut back regularly to encourage bushy, flowering stems.

Summer Sunshine

Mixing flowering annuals with plants that have interesting foliage can give even the most stalwart of old faithfuls a new look. Here, zinnias and trailing gazanias are combined with the striking foliage of golden marjoram and golden feverfew to create a planting that instantly spells out summer. The gazanias and zinnias both need sun for their flowers to open; the flowers of golden marjoram, however, are best removed to promote its fine display of leaves.

Gazania (*Gazania uniflora*)
A beautiful combination of silver leaves and yellow flowers.

PRACTICAL MATTERS

SOIL
Plant in a well-drained potting mixture of medium nutritional value.

SITE
Place in a sunny position.

WATERING
Take care not to overwater. Feed once a week.

PLANTS
Grow two gazanias, four zinnias, two golden marjoram, and two golden feverfew in a 75cm-(30in-) long, yellow-painted, wooden window box.

Blue Backdrop
❧ Planted boxes need not always sit on window sills. This box is set against the base of an old, disused door. The door's deep blue colouring gives the yellows and golds of the summer flowers tremendous strength.

SHIMMERING FLOWERS AND FOLIAGE

SILVER FOLIAGE AND WHITE FLOWERS combine to create a delicate, shimmering effect in a simple, plastic, white window box. This summery scheme is best placed on a low window sill that sees plenty of sun, and is also situated well away from the road – pollution does not suit silver-leaved plants and quickly covers white flowers with a dirty sheen. The zonal pelargoniums and the marguerites need deadheading to encourage a continuous display.

Other white-flowered plants could replace the pelargoniums: white varieties of bellflower, petunia, pansy, busy Lizzy, and tobacco plants all give a spectacular summer show. Choose a combination of plants that gives interesting contrasts.

Santolina (*Santolina neapolitana* 'Sulphurea')
Pale yellow flowers appear above the silver, aromatic leaves in mid summer.

Senecio (*Senecio maritima*)
Treated as an annual, its fine, silvery foliage grows very quickly and may need an occasional trim.

White and Silver

❆ The plain, white, plastic window box sets off the various leaf shapes and textures provided by the silver plants in this bright arrangement, and yet at the same time reflects the pure white of the pelargoniums and marguerites. Notice how the pale yellow santolina flowers add just a hint of colour variation.

Zonal pelargonium
(*Pelargonium* 'Modesty')
A pretty, pure white form of one of the most reliable of annuals.

Marguerite
(*Chrysanthemum frutescens*)
A small-flowered variety, ideal for growing in a window box.

PRACTICAL MATTERS

SOIL
Plant in a well-drained potting mixture of medium nutritional value.

SITE
Place in a sunny position.

WATERING
Water well, but do not allow to become soggy at any time.

PLANTS
Grow three zonal pelargoniums, two marguerites, two senecio, two southernwoods, one santolina, and four plecostachys in an 80cm- (32in-) long, white, plastic window box.

Southernwood
(*Artemisia abrotanum*)
A semi-evergreen shrub with strongly fragrant foliage.

Plecostachys
(*Plecostachys serpyllifolium*)
The delicate, silver foliage of this small-leaved, tender perennial cascades over the window box.

THE LAST OF SUMMER

WHILE WE TEND TO THINK of annuals in terms of the flowers they produce and their flowering time, a great many species and varieties also have leaves that can be used to great effect. Three of the varieties in this planting boast attractive foliage, although the variegated nasturtiums with their wonderful leaves splashed with cream have rather taken over the front of the arrangement.

The coleus, seen towards the back, are grown solely for their leaves, which come in a startling array of colours. Begonias have the bonus of both decorative flowers and foliage. Their strongly veined, heart-shaped leaves make a bold statement in any planting, and their flowers appear for months. Both the begonias and nasturtiums flower particularly well in autumn when many other annuals tail off.

Petunia *(Petunia*
x *hybrida* 'Red Satin')
The red flowers are not
blemished by bad weather.

Rampant Growers
All the annuals in this planting – especially the nasturtiums – are vigorous growers, so do not put them in an interesting or decorative window box. At the height of the display the flowers and foliage will conceal the sides.

PRACTICAL MATTERS

SOIL
Plant in a well-drained potting mixture of medium nutritional value.

SITE
Place in a sunny site that is not too exposed to wind.

WATERING
Water to keep the soil just moist, but not soggy. Do not overfeed.

PLANTS
Grow five nasturtiums, three coleus, three tuberous begonias, and three petunias in a 70cm- (28in-) long, plastic window box.

Begonia *(Begonia × tuberhybrida)*
The apricot-orange flowers complement
the other colours in the planting.

Coleus *(Coleus blumei)*
A half-hardy annual grown
for its colourful foliage.

Nasturtium
*(Tropaeolum
majus* 'Alaska')
The edible flowers
can be used to
decorate salads.

HAZE OF HEATHERS

WITH THE ENORMOUS RANGE of varieties available, it is possible to have heathers in flower every month of the year. They do have very specific growing needs – acid soil and moist conditions – but by growing them in a container, you can easily meet these requirements, encouraging the plants to perform well. *Calluna vulgaris*, the species in this white window box, has had many varieties developed from it, with flowers that vary from pink, through purple and lilac, to white. The spires of flowers appear from late summer until early winter, depending on the variety, and are excellent in combination with conifers, which enjoy the same conditions.

When these heathers have finished flowering, cut off the flower heads. With its mixed foliage, this planting will continue to look attractive throughout the winter. Otherwise, replace these heathers with varieties of *Erica* X *darleyensis,* which have pink, cream, or red flowers during the winter months.

Heather (*Calluna vulgaris* vars.) A hardy evergreen, flowering from late summer to early winter.

Moorland Flowers

The misty colours of the heathers (RIGHT) are backed by silver-grey clouds of cypress foliage. To make the flowers last, give the heathers a weekly water spray to simulate the conditions of their native moorland.

PRACTICAL MATTERS

SOIL

Plant in an ericaceous (acid) potting mixture, peat, and sharp sand (proportions 3:2:1).

SITE

Place in a sunny position, which is sheltered from cold winds.

WATERING

Water to keep the plants moist during non-frosty weather, and give a liquid feed once a month.

PLANTS

Grow five Lawson's cypress, five heathers, and four ivies in a 75cm- (30in-) long, plastic window box.

Lawson's cypress
(*Chamaecyparis lawsoniana* 'Nana Glauca')
A slow-growing conifer.

Ivy (*Hedera helix* 'Elegance')
A trailing, silver-edged variety.

Clipped Hedge

✄ Clip the conifers in this window box (ABOVE) to make a miniature hedge at the back of the arrangement. This is best done from mid summer to autumn, when the new growth is established. Thereafter, give them an occasional clip, perhaps twice a year, to keep them neat and tidy.

ARRAY OF EVERGREENS

A SURPRISINGLY WIDE SELECTION of evergreen plants have interestingly shaped or attractively coloured foliage, which makes them useful for year-round container plantings, and winter arrangements in particular. Extremely harsh winters can be a problem for plants in containers, but a small selection can withstand the icy, winter onslaught. Those with interesting foliage include abelia, cotoneaster, Cornish heath, euonymus, holly, calico bush, privet, box, ivy, lavender, pieris, periwinkle, and many conifers: false cypress, juniper, spruce, pine, yew, and Eastern hemlock, to name just a few possibilities.

✗ For an amusing winter arrangement, plant decorative cabbages and evergreen skimmia in autumn (SEE PAGES 164-5). Their bright colourful leaves will bring pleasure through the winter months. Like edible cabbages, the decorative forms eventually bolt, so you will have to pull them out in spring.

✗ Containers, too, can suffer in very low temperatures, especially the terracotta and glazed ceramic ones. Some are frost-proofed when they are made, so if you live in a frost-prone area, check before you buy.

PRACTICAL MATTERS

SOIL
Plant in a slightly acid potting mixture.
SITE
Place in a sheltered, sunny or semi-shady position.
WATERING
Water occasionally. Do not water when temperatures fall below freezing.
PLANTS
Grow three skimmias, five senecio, and four winter cherries in an 80cm- (32in-) long, wooden window box.

Winter cherry
(Solanum capsicastrum)
Varieties with yellow and white berries are available, too.

Winter Buds and Berries

✗ A white, wooden window box makes an excellent foil for this mix of dark greens, silvers, and orange. In temperate climates the planting will give a bright display from late autumn to early summer, with the skimmias producing pink buds throughout the winter and white flowers in the summer. This planting is not suitable for very cold regions.

Thuja *(Thuja orientalis* 'Aurea Nana')
If left to mature, these compact, golden balls of leaves will eventually become conical.

Mexican orange blossom *(Choisya ternata* 'Sundance')
The leaves stay golden all year. Scented flowers open in late spring.

Juniper *(Juniperus conferta)*
A low, spreading conifer, ideal for growing at the front of a window box.

Euonymus *(Euonymus fortunei* 'Emerald 'n' Gold')
The glowing gold and green foliage is tinged pink in winter.

Skimmia *(Skimmia japonica* 'Rubella')
For a good crop of berries, most skimmias need a male pollinator nearby.

Senecio *(Senecio maritima)*
Usually grown as annuals, these silver-leaved plants often survive mild winters.

Golden Glow

✄ A honey-coloured, reconstituted stone window box supports a variety of golden and green-leaved shrubs. Particular care over the positioning of the plants creates an arresting, overall shape. This arrangement looks attractive throughout the year.

PRACTICAL MATTERS

SOIL
Plant in a potting mixture of medium nutritional value.
SITE
Suitable for any position.
WATERING
Water once a fortnight during winter, unless temperatures fall below freezing. In summer, keep the soil moist, and feed once a month.
PLANTS
Grow two thujas, two Mexican orange blossoms, three euonymus, and one juniper in a 105cm- (38in-) long, reconstituted stone window box.

TERRACOTTA BAROQUE

WITH ITS DECORATIVE, pale blue swirls and owl-like feet, this fascinating window box suggests a planting with an unusual colour scheme. Although many colours would work well in it, these apricots, pinks, maroons, and rusts are especially effective. The apricot hyacinths pick up the colour of the container and blend surprisingly well with the pinks. The maroon and rust auriculas accentuate the pink of the tulips, and the touch of yellow heightens the effect of the other colours, bringing the whole scheme to life.

SPRING SCENTS

This is an arrangement that appeals to the nose as well as delights the eye. Hyacinths have a perfume that seems to epitomize spring, although it can be almost too strong. Auriculas release a sweet, fresh scent, slightly reminiscent of early flag irises. More delicate but quite pervasive is the smell of the polyanthus, and even the tulips have a light, sweet, peppery perfume.

TENDER CARE

All primulas are excellent for growing in containers, although the auriculas must be protected from rain and frost to flower perfectly. The shelter of a window recess provides an ideal site. Care will be rewarded, for few garden flowers have such extraordinary yet beautiful colour combinations.

Hyacinth
(*Hyacinthus orientalis* 'Oranje Boven')
Like most hyacinths, this variety has a delicious scent.

Polyanthus
(*Primula vulgaris* hybrids)
Ideal for growing with spring bulbs in window boxes.

PRACTICAL MATTERS

SOIL
Plant in a lightweight potting mixture of medium nutritional value.

SITE
Place in a sunny or semi-shady position, sheltered from excessive rain.

WATERING
Keep barely moist, but not dry.

PLANTS
Grow seven hyacinths, six auriculas, ten tulips, and three polyanthus in a 68cm- (27in-) long, handmade, terracotta window box.

Clay Swirls
Ideally, the box is best placed up so that it can be seen to its maximum advantage. Hyacinths, tulips, auriculas, and polyanthus vie for attention in this decorative, handmade window box. I avoided using any trailing plants, such as periwinkle or ivy, as they would cover the front of the container and conceal its striking pattern.

Tulip *(Tulipa* 'Peach Blossom')
A pretty, double variety which
flowers in early spring.

Auricula
(Primula auricula)
These alpine
primulas are
available in an
extraordinary
range of
colours.

Ornamental terracotta
The colour wash slip on
this highly ornate window
box helps soften the harsh
colour of new terracotta.

FAVOURED HELLEBORES

HELLEBORES ARE ENJOYING a revival in popularity, and a deserved one, too. Among the few perennials that flower in winter and early spring, they are also invaluable for container plantings at this sparse time of year. Here, I have used *Helleborus* x *sternii*; its gorgeous, green flowers last two months in late winter and early spring, coinciding with the first tulips.

✿ The Christmas rose *(Helleborus niger)* is the most popular hellebore, and the first to bloom, its pure white flowers often appearing in time for Christmas. The Lenten rose *(Helleborus orientalis)* flowers later, but offers a variation in colour, ranging from white and green through to deep, plummy pink, often with delicately spotted petals. Both species grow successfully in containers.

PRACTICAL MATTERS
•
SOIL
Plant in a well-drained potting mixture of high nutritional value, mixed with two large handfuls of leafmould.
SITE
Place in a semi-shady site for the best results.
WATERING
Keep just moist, and do not allow the potting mixture to become too dry.
PLANTS
Grow four hellebores and fifteen tulips in a 60cm- (24in-) long, terracotta window box.
•

Hellebore
(Helleborus x *sternii)*
A reasonably hardy hellebore.
In colder climates grow
Helleborus orientalis instead.

Waterlily tulip
(*Tulipa* 'Ancilla')
A low-growing
kaufmanniana
hybrid, favoured
for early spring
plantings.

China-like Flowers
↘ A simple, yet effective,
early spring planting of
hellebores and tulips
growing in a decorative,
terracotta window box.
The striped tulips are an
interesting foil to the
hellebores. Position the
window box where you
can appreciate the delicacy
of the hellebores' almost
china-like flowers.

POTS

THE TRADITIONAL flower pot, with sides that slope outwards slightly, has been used in gardens since the Roman times. Until recently, this type of pot was always made out of terracotta, a once-fired, porous, red clay, which is very attractive but can crack and flake with weathering in very cold temperatures. Sometimes, elements are added to the clay before it is fired to make it frost-proof. If you live in a cold area where frosts are likely, make sure that the terracotta you buy has been treated in this way.

✻ Decorative, glazed ceramic pots, often from the Far East, Italy, and Spain, are now widely available. They come in a beautiful range of colours, but tend to be even less frost-proof, as glaze can easily crack. However, many are frost-resistant so always check before you buy.

✻ As terracotta is a highly porous material, it absorbs a lot of moisture from the potting mixture; the moisture then evaporates into the air. Because of this, plants in terracotta pots require more frequent watering than plants in plastic pots. It is also advisable to soak terracotta pots thoroughly before planting them up, as it is essential that new plants have a plentiful supply of water to start them off.

─── PATINA OF AGE ───

Over the last thirty years, plastic pots have become widely used. They are cheaper than terracotta, frost-proof and, because they are not porous, absorb less moisture from the soil. But this means that they do not take on a patina of age, and it is this patina which, I think, makes terracotta pots so beautiful and so much more interesting to plant up. If I use terracotta, I

CHINESE CERAMICS
Set against a sea of lavender, blue-glazed Chinese pots of zonal pelargoniums (ABOVE) stand grandly on the plinths bordering a flight of brick and stone steps.

PAINT EFFECTS
Sun-loving herbs (LEFT) grow in a selection of colour-washed terracotta pots, an effect achieved by applying a dilute, water-based paint to the outsides of the pots.

usually paint the outside of the pot with a coat of live yoghurt to speed up the weathering process. Placed in a shady position, it soon becomes covered with moss; if it is in a sunny spot, grey-white patches develop. Pots made of stone or reconstituted stone can also be weathered in this way.

✻ For a change from the traditional colour of terracotta, which tends to be on the harsh side, you can give pots a colour-wash (LEFT), by applying a wash of dilute, water-based paint. I find that the blue-green colours and terracotta pinks are the most effective − try to avoid yellows as they do not work as well as the other colours.

─── POT COLLECTION ───

Small pots can often make more of an impact on a terrace or patio if they are arranged in a group. They also look stunning on an old wire-work plant stand (SEE PAGE 127). They need not be exactly the same design or size. Indeed, the grouping usually looks more effective if it consists of different-sized and shaped pots. You can also have fun mixing and matching the different materials from which they are made. Stone, reconstituted stone, and terracotta all look fine side-by-side. More unusual is a mixture of glazed, ceramic pots, well-designed plastic, or fibreglass containers in sympathetic colours, and metal pots with subtle sheens; they can also complement each other, giving a sophisticated look.

✻ I find that pots are also useful in herbaceous borders. Filled with flowering plants or colourful foliage, pots can add interest to a patch that lacks colour at a particular time of year. They can also help to introduce a little height to an area with low-growing plants or a newly planted plot.

JUST TULIPS

S IMPLE, SPRING BULBS, such as tulips, hyacinths, crocuses, and narcissi, are easy to grow in pots, and indeed any other sort of container. They are not demanding and the cold rarely affects them. Only high winds and torrential rain, when the tulips are in bloom, can mar their brilliant display.

✿ Tulips have been highly valued for many centuries by gardeners, encouraging the bulb hybridizers to develop more and more forms. Bulb growers specify whether the bulbs are early, mid, or late season, but it is always a little hit and miss. To ensure that all the flowers in an arrangement come out at once, it is best to grow only one variety in each pot, unless you know the varieties well.

—— LAYERED PLANTING PLAN ——

Plant the bulbs in mid to late autumn, as soon as you get them home from the garden centre. Do not allow them to dry out. Provided they are in good condition, you can plant them up until early winter. Expect them to flower four to five months after planting. To get best results, plant fresh bulbs each autumn and move the old bulbs into the garden.

✿ For a dense tulip planting and magnificent show, plant the bulbs in two layers. This way you will pack twice as many bulbs in, and therefore have twice as many flowers later, giving a spectacular display. Here, I have risked growing two different varieties together: a dramatic yellow and red striped parrot tulip with an attractive, deep-red, fringed form. I have grown both these forms in the past and I know that they should flower simultaneously.

✎ PLANTING A POT OF BULBS ✎

1 *Place clean crocks on the base of the container to cover the drainage holes, and add charcoal to keep the soil sweet. Next, firm in a slightly alkaline potting mixture to within 20cm (8in) from the top of the container. Place the 'Flaming Parrot' bulbs on this, 2cm (1in) apart.*

2 *Sprinkle more of the potting mixture over the bulbs until they are nearly covered. Place a layer of 'Redwing' tulip bulbs above the gaps between the first layer. Fill with potting mixture to 2cm (1in) below the top of the pot to facilitate watering. Water lightly.*

Perfect Partners

Tulips come in an enormous range of flower shapes and colours, presenting the enterprising gardener with endless opportunities to create eye-catching combinations. With their yellow and red colouring, but varied flower form and difference in height, 'Flaming Parrot' and 'Redwing' make excellent companions. Both are late-flowering hybrids.

PRACTICAL MATTERS

SOIL
Plant in a well-drained, slightly alkaline potting mixture.

SITE
Place in a sunny or shady position.

WATERING
Keep the potting mixture just moist, but do not water in extremely cold conditions.

PLANTS
Grow twelve 'Redwing' tulip bulbs and fifteen 'Flaming Parrot' bulbs in a 30cm- (12in-) diameter, ceramic pot.

Parrot Tulip (*Tulipa* 'Flaming Parrot')
The parrot tulips are distinguished by their frilly-edged petals. All flower in late spring.

Tulip (*Tulipa* 'Redwing')
A deep red, incurved flower with fringed edges to its petals.

Pink Tulip Picture

'Picture', distinguished by its pale pink, waxy flowers is an especially attractive tulip for an old, weathered, terracotta pot. I planted twenty bulbs in this pot, which measures 30cm (12in) in diameter, and then covered the potting mixture with moss.

TOWERS FOR FLOWERS

WITH DAFFODILS, SCILLAS, AND GRAPE HYACINTHS as firm favourites, conventional spring plantings are usually a combination of yellows and blues. I wanted a change. These dramatic, ceramic towers seem to me the antithesis of spring. Covered in a black glaze splashed with brown and petrol-blue, they look most effective with a planting of Persian buttercups and broom.

✀ Persian buttercups have small, double, peony-like flowers, and are in the same family as the common buttercup. In mild districts, given protection from frost in winter, they bear their flowers in late spring. Small plants placed outside after the frosts have finished will not flower until early to mid summer.

✀ The broom used here is also semi-hardy, needing the same frost protection as the Persian buttercups. In spring, it produces a long succession of bright yellow, sweetly scented blooms, lasting for weeks. A trailing, curly leaved ivy is planted in all the towers to offset the bright colours.

Persian buttercup
(*Ranunculus asiaticus*)
Available either as one colour, or in a mixture of reds, oranges, yellows, pinks, and whites, the flowers can be plain or striped.

PRACTICAL MATTERS

SOIL
Plant the Persian buttercups in a rich potting mixture and leafmould. The broom and ivy need a well-drained potting mixture of low nutritional value.

SITE
Place in a sunny, sheltered position.

WATERING
Keep the Persian buttercups well watered, almost to the point of being soggy, the others should be kept just moist.

PLANTS
Grow six Persian buttercups and four ivies in one of the larger towers (measuring 50cm/20in across), one broom and four ivies in the other large one, and then two ivies alone in the smaller tower (measuring 30cm/12in).

Ivy (*Hedera helix* 'Parsley Crested') Distinguished by a mass of light green, frilly leaves.

Pebbled Setting
A sunny combination of Persian buttercups, broom, and ivy that looks cheerful even in dull weather. Place this arrangement on a pebbled area, or stone or grey brick pavings. An ivy-clad wall would provide the perfect background.

Broom (*Cytisus* x *spachianus*) The sweet perfume of this broom from the Canary Islands carries well on the air.

Ceramic towers
Handmade pots with a matt black, brown, and petrol-blue glaze make striking containers for plants.

ELEGANT COMPANIONS

O NLY A HANDFUL of spring bulbs grow to a good size. They include Solomon's seal (BELOW), which flowers in late spring and early summer and likes a shaded or semi-shaded site, and the crown imperials (RIGHT). Grown in three colours – yellow, orange, or deep red – the crown imperials are at their best in mid to late spring in a semi-shady or sunny spot. While the crown imperials are very imposing, the Solomon's seal is cool, quiet, and elegant. Both bear their flowers well above ground level, so they look best if they are underplanted with a mound of low-growing plants in complementary colours that flower at the same time. Pansies and forget-me-nots fulfil this role well, but double daisies or aubretia are viable alternatives. The crown imperials and the Solomon's seal flower in their pots for several years. After flowering, let the soil dry out and the foliage die down.

— WEATHERED TERRACOTTA —

Both these arrangements are planted in swagged terracotta pots. To hasten the weathering process, I painted yoghurt on the pot holding the crown imperials. The yoghurt attracted moss and lichen, which look especially effective on pots with raised patterns.

Solomon's seal
(*Polygonatum* x *hybridum*)
The white, hanging, trumpet-shaped flowers are flushed green.

Forget-me-not
(*Myosotis* 'Blue Ball')
The clear blue flowers fade to pink. A variety best grown as a biennial.

PRACTICAL MATTERS
•
SOIL
Plant in a well-drained potting mixture of high nutritional value.
SITE
Place in a semi-shady site.
WATERING
Keep just moist in winter and spring. Do not water in frosty weather.
PLANTS
Grow two clumps of Solomon's seal, and five forget-me-nots in a 38cm- (15in-) diameter, swagged, terracotta pot.
•

Dappled Shade
⚘ The graceful, arching stems of the Solomon's seal rise sedately from a froth of soft blue forget-me-nots, its white flowers nodding above. One of my favourite combinations, this subtle planting looks special in the dappled shade of a deciduous tree that has just come into leaf.

Crown imperial
(*Fritillaria imperialis* 'Lutea')
Plant the bulbs in autumn for blooms in mid spring.

Pansy (*Violax wittrockiana* Universal Series)
A beautiful, apricot strain flowering from early spring to mid summer.

PRACTICAL MATTERS

SOIL
Plant in a well-drained potting mixture of medium nutritional value.

SITE
Place in a sunny or semi-shady position.

WATERING
Water to keep the soil just moist. After flowering, let the soil dry out.

PLANTS
Grow eight crown imperial bulbs and six pansies in a 42cm- (17in-) diameter, terracotta pot.

Regal Golds
⚹ The combination of yellow crown imperials and orange pansies works well in the weathered, terracotta pot. Unfortunately, crown imperials have a rank odour, so place the pot where it can be seen, but not smelt.

FLAMBOYANT AZALEAS

AZALEAS AND OTHER RHODODENDRONS are extremely easy to grow in containers. In their native habitats they are woodland plants, so they perform best in acid soil and in dappled shade; they do not like very hot, dry, summer weather. Ideally, you should grow them by themselves, or with another permanent planting so that you avoid disturbing their roots too frequently.

——— SPRING FLOWERS ———

Most azaleas flower for just a few weeks in late spring, but they are most useful for filling an awkward gap in the gardening calendar, after the bulb season has finished but before the summer flowers begin. Their flowers, which often smother the plant, cover an enormous range of colours. Remove them once they have died so that the plant will put its energy into new growth, instead of producing seed. Feed once they have finished flowering, but only until mid summer, otherwise too much late, soft growth will develop.

——— WINTER WATERING ———

All rhododendrons are shallow-rooted, so they dry out easily. It is important to make sure that the potting mixture is always just moist, even during the winter. Rain reaches the roots of deciduous azaleas during the winter, as they have no leaves to shelter the soil, but evergreen rhododendrons will still need to be watered regularly.

PRACTICAL MATTERS
•
SOIL
Plant in a well-drained, acid potting mixture, with added leafmould.
SITE
Place in a semi-shady site.
WATERING
Keep the soil just moist throughout the year. After flowering, feed weekly until mid summer.
PLANTS
Grow one azalea and four ferns in each 42cm- (17in-) diameter, terracotta pot.
•

• **Azalea** (*Rhododendron* 'Fedora')
An evergreen variety with phlox-pink blossoms.

Hot Clashing Colours

✄ Azalea flowers cover an enormous range of colours. I find the more violent shades work well together. These three grow with a ruff of ferns that favour exactly the same site, soil, and watering conditions. As each azalea grows larger, you can transfer the entire root ball, together with the ferns, into a larger pot.

• **Azalea** (*Rhododendron* 'Vuyk's Scarlet') Brilliant red flowers smother this evergreen variety at the height of its flowering season.

• **Azalea** (*Rhododendron* 'Konigen Emma') One of the Mollis hybrids, grown for its colourful autumn foliage as well as the spring flowers.

• **Fern** (*Polystichum setiferum*) A species that stays evergreen throughout the winter months.

SPRING NARCISSI

Double daffodil
(*Narcissus* 'Tahiti')
A robust form, with
double flowers and
a slight scent.

POTS LOOK MOST EFFECTIVE filled to overflowing with spring bulbs. Narcissi are among the easiest to grow. I find that it is best to plant just one variety in each pot – you can still contrast the various flower forms and colours by having several pots planted up, each displaying a different flower. I can never resist growing at least one pot of a fragrant variety: the paperwhites and pheasant eye have a sweet scent but, to me, the perfume of the jonquils is the most delicious. Plant the bulbs in autumn, layering them (SEE PAGE 34) for maximum visual impact.

Shades of Spring
The sky-blues of these frost-proof ceramic pots, planted with the clear yellows of four varieties of narcissus, epitomize the colours of a spring day. Experiment with different varieties, choosing from the enormous range of colours: pink, apricot, and white, as well as yellow and orange.

Large-cupped daffodil
(*Narcissus* 'Salmon Trout')
As the flowers age, the perianths turn pink.

Cyclamineus daffodil
(*Narcissus* 'Tête-à-Tête')
A small form with reflexed petals and a good perfume.

PRACTICAL MATTERS

SOIL
Plant in a well-drained potting mixture of medium to rich nutritional value.

SITE
Place in any site, but avoid bright sunlight to prolong flowering.

WATERING
Keep just moist, but never allow to become soggy.

PLANTS
Grow 24 bulbs in each 25-35cm- (10-14in-) diameter pot, and cover potting mixture with moss.

Double daffodil
(*Narcissus* 'Yellow Cheerfulness')
A scented variety.

ROSES ALL SUMMER

THE BEAUTY OF THE ROSE is indisputable: it has a sumptuous look that epitomizes summer. However, the plant on which the flowers grow is not such a beauty. For much of the year the rose bush is a gangly, awkward plant with unattractive stems covered by vicious thorns, and leaves that are prone to disease.

By growing roses in containers, you can bring them into the limelight when they are at their best, and keep them out of sight when they are not. Only the smaller roses do well in containers: polyanthas, cluster-flowered varieties, and miniatures. The larger varieties will never produce an abundance of blooms.

Rose (*Rosa* 'Yellow Cushion') The flowers have a slight scent.

PRACTICAL MATTERS

SOIL
Plant in a well-drained potting mixture of high nutritional value.

SITE
Place in a sunny site.

WATERING
Water well and feed weekly with a flower-promoting fertilizer.

PLANTS
Grow one 'The Fairy', in one 42cm- (17in-) diameter, frost-proofed glazed pot, and two 'Yellow Cushion' in the other.

Rose (*Rosa* 'The Fairy') A polyantha that flowers later than other roses, but compensates for this by continuing until winter.

Pair of Roses
✿ Pink and yellow are not an obvious colour combination, but they work well together here. This arrangement would suit a contemporary setting.

PINK PELARGONIUMS

PELARGONIUMS ARE THE MOST REWARDING plants to grow. They flower abundantly, require little attention, and do extremely well in containers. In a sunny or semi-shady position with plenty of light, they grow quickly into substantial plants, producing plentiful flushes of flowers from early summer until the first frosts. They frequently survive light frosts and go on producing flowers well into the winter. However, the combination of late cold spells and damp usually kills them. This is no bad thing, because they tend to get woody and unshapely in their second flowering season, and usually produce fewer flowers. It is, therefore, best to grow new plants every year, either from seed sown in late winter (for flowering that summer), or from cuttings taken in late summer, for flowering the following summer. Both methods are relatively easy. (For details on the different propagation techniques, SEE PAGES 182-3.)

Different types and varieties of pelargonium grow well together in the same container, provided they are equally vigorous. Some of the smaller-growing varieties can become swamped by the larger, more robust forms, so it is advisable to avoid combining them.

✁ PLANTING A POT ✁

1 *Place crocks in the base of the pot, then firm in potting mixture to about 10cm (4in) below the rim. With the plants still in their pots, arrange pelargoniums in the centre, and the verbena around the edge so it trails over the side of the pot.*

2 *Tap the plants out of their pots (before planting, water them to soak the roots) and gently loosen the base. Firm into position, adding potting mixture so that its final level is 4cm (1¹/₂in) below the pot rim. Remove dead leaves, and water.*

Zonal pelargonium
(*Pelargonium* 'Fraicher Beauty')
The perfectly formed, pale pink flowers are double.

Regal pelargonium
(*Pelargonium* 'Langley Smith')
A small-flowered variety with white petals marked carmine-pink.

PRACTICAL MATTERS

•

SOIL

Plant in a well-drained potting mixture of medium to rich nutritional value.

SITE

Place in sun or semi-shade.

WATERING

Keep on the dry side of moist, and feed with a weak liquid fertilizer every two weeks.

PLANTS

Grow two regal pelargoniums, three zonal pelargoniums, and four verbena in a 52cm- (21in-) diameter, terracotta pot.

•

Zonal pelargonium
(*Pelargonium* 'Rio')
The intense, pink flowers have even darker centres.

Verbena (*Verbena* x *hybrida* 'Silver Anne')
A sweet-scented variety.

Shades of Pink

I have chosen regal pelargoniums with white, pale pink, and deep pink flowers to meld with zonal pelargoniums – a pale pink variety with a deep pink eye, and an ice-pink form faintly flushed with deeper pink. The verbenas are in a similar hue: a deep, but not harsh, pink. All the colours look striking against the green leaves.

Regal pelargonium
(*Pelargonium* 'Tip Top Duet')
A variety with white and pink petals blotched with burgundy.

45

TENDER, FLOWERING SHRUBS

THESE TWO SHRUBS – a plumbago and an abutilon – give a continuous display of flowers throughout the summer and autumn. Both are tender, however, so you must treat them as annuals, unless you are gardening in a frost-free climate, or have a cool conservatory in which to overwinter them. They grow extremely fast and will give a good show of flowers during the summer in which they are planted. The plumbago shown here produces a succession of pure sky-blue flowers from early summer until early winter. In ideal conditions, it will grow to reach 3m (10ft) high. The abutilon has much the same attributes. It carries a profusion of yellow, bell-shaped flowers flushed with peach for several months and grows large in one season. It is also frost-tender.

Tender Care

❅ This plumbago is supported by a wigwam of three bamboo stakes. As it grows, tie in the main stem and a few of the side shoots, but do not cut it back or its flowering will be curtailed. If overwintering, prune well to promote new flowering growth in spring. The gypsophila is planted in the side cups of an upturned chimney pot.

PRACTICAL MATTERS

SOIL
Plant in a well-drained potting mixture of high nutritional value.
SITE
Place in a sheltered, sunny site.
WATERING
Water well. Feed once a week.
PLANTS
Grow one plumbago and five gypsophila in a 38cm- (15in-) diameter, chimney pot.

Plumbago
(Plumbago auriculata)
A tender, fast-growing climber with trusses of blue flowers.

Gypsophila
(Gypsophila repens 'Dorothy Teacher')
Produces delicate powder puffs of little flowers.

Abutilon *(Abutilon* x *hybridum* 'Golden Fleece') Although other abutilons also grow well in pots, this variety has the longest flowering season.

Miniature snapdragon *(Antirrhinum pulverulentum)* Small, trailing stems become covered with creamy yellow flowers.

PRACTICAL MATTERS

SOIL
Plant in a well-drained potting mixture of high nutritional value.
SITE
Place in a sunny, sheltered position.
WATERING
Water well throughout the growing season and feed once a week.
PLANTS
Grow one abutilon and four miniature snapdragons in a 32cm- (13in-) diameter, terracotta pot.

Yellow Scheme
⚘ The creamy yellow, bell-shaped flowers and large, soft green leaves of abutilon are offset by the froth of miniature snapdragons growing around the base and down the side of the container. Pale yellow marigolds and petunias would also make an effective underplanting.

VARIEGATED PELARGONIUMS

PELARGONIUMS, OFTEN INCORRECTLY CALLED GERANIUMS, are rewarding plants to grow in containers. They put on a continuous show of flowers from the beginning of summer until the first frosts of autumn or early winter – in warmer, dryer climates they often continue to flower through the winter. As a bonus, many of the varieties have beautifully patterned leaves, which are sometimes scented.

Zonal pelargonium
(Pelargonium 'Dolly Varden')
Handsome green, purple, and cream leaves with scarlet flowers.

PELARGONIUM VARIETIES

Four types of pelargonium are grown in gardens: zonal, ivy-leaved, scented-leaved, and regal. The most common are the zonal pelargoniums, distinguished by their rounded, fleshy leaves with a variegated band. Their heads of small, single or double flowers vary in colour from red and orange, through pink and mauve, to white. The ivy-leaved varieties have single or double flowers, small, ivy-like leaves, and a trailing habit, which makes them ideal for hanging baskets. Regal pelargoniums are grown for their large, showy flowers although, unfortunately, they are easily damaged by wet weather. The scented-leaved pelargoniums are valued for their foliage. Their insignificant flowers are best removed to encourage the growth of the leaves, noted for their lemon, apple, rose, pine, or mint fragrances.

☀ Pelargoniums perform best in a sunny site. When the young plants are 15cm (6in) tall, remove the leading growing tip to make them bush out well. Deadhead regularly to encourage flowering.

Patterned Foliage
☀ Four pelargoniums, chosen for their striking leaf patterns as well as their flowers, grow in this handmade, terracotta pot. The three zonal varieties have a distinct band on their leaves. The scented-leaved variety at the front is grown for its aromatic, cream-edged leaves.

Scented-leaved pelargonium
(Pelargonium 'Lady Plymouth')
When bruised, the pretty leaves of this variety exude a delicious, sharp, lemon scent.

Strategic Planning
☀ Plant 'Lady Plymouth', the scented pelargonium, at the front of the planting so that passers-by gently bruise the foliage and release its scent. The other three pelargoniums all have a bushy habit, which introduces height and bulk to this luxuriant arrangement.

• Zonal pelargonium
(Pelargonium 'Frank Headley')
Pink flowers appear above the
cream-edged green leaves.

• Zonal pelargonium
(Pelargonium 'Mrs Quilter')
The lime-green leaves with
chestnut patterning and the
salmon-pink flowers make
a stunning combination.

PRACTICAL MATTERS

SOIL
Plant in a well-drained potting mixture of
medium nutritional value.

SITE
Flowering is most prolific in a sunny site,
although the plants still grow well in a
semi-shady position.

WATERING
In hot, sunny weather water daily, but do
not allow the roots to become soggy –
they rot easily. Feed lightly once a week.

PLANTS
Grow three zonal pelargoniums and one
scented-leaved pelargonium in a 30cm-
(12in-) diameter, terracotta pot.

LILIES AND BELLFLOWERS

ILIES ARE REWARDING PLANTS to grow in pots. They produce an abundance of spectacular flowers that last for several weeks in summer, yet their demands – a sunny or semi-shady site and a rich, potting mixture – are not difficult to meet. For summer flowers, plant the lily bulbs in late autumn, or during the winter in areas not too exposed to extreme cold. Once their flowering shoots appear in late spring, introduce some lower-growing annuals or perennials between and around them, so that their trumpet-shaped blooms eventually rise from a mound of flowers that complements both their colour and their elegant form.

Lily (*Lilium* 'Connecticut King') This variety carries gorgeous, upward-facing blooms on its 1m- (36in-) high stems in the early summer.

Bellflower (*Campanula carpatica*) A clump-forming perennial with long-lasting flowers in summer.

A Fitting Base
✗ A deep blue, glazed, Chinese pot provides an elegant base for the mound of bellflowers and the regal stems of lily blooms, which soar high above them.

PRACTICAL MATTERS

SOIL
Grow in a very well-drained potting mixture, enriched with compost and leafmould.

SITE
Place in a sunny or semi-shady site.

WATERING
Keep the potting mixture moist, but not soggy, and give a weekly liquid feed during the growing season.

PLANTS
Grow ten lilies and five bellflowers in a 40cm- (16in-) diameter pot.

PALACE PURPLE

TOO OFTEN, WE NEGLECT THE PLANTS that have interesting leaf shapes and colours, in favour of those that produce attractive flowers. Here, as a change from flowering summer annuals, I have planted a group of showy foliage perennials. Easy to grow in semi-shade, they will look good right through summer and autumn for years to come. *Tovara virginiana* 'Painter's Palette', and *Leucothöe fontanesiana* 'Rainbow', also perennials with wonderful leaves, are other possibilities for this long-lasting and colourful melange.

PRACTICAL MATTERS

SOIL
Plant in a well-drained potting mixture of high nutritional value.
SITE
Place in a semi-shady or shady site.
WATERING
Water all the plants well, especially the houttuynia.
PLANTS
Grow one heuchera, one houttuynia, and one pick-a-back plant in a 48cm- (19in-) diameter, terracotta pot.

Aura of Elegance
✠ The deep purple colouring of the heuchera leaves is accentuated by the speckled golds of the pick-a-back plant and the multicoloured, houttuynia leaves.

Houttuynia (*Houttuynia cordata* 'Chamaeleon')
The pretty, coloured leaves have a pungent, orange scent.

Heuchera (*Heuchera* 'Palace Purple')
The pretty purple foliage is sometimes used in flower arrangements.

Pick-a-back plant (*Tolmiea menziesii*)
A perennial that is easy to propagate, as new plants grow from the leaf-stem joints.

CASCADING DIASCIAS

SINGLE SPECIES PLANTINGS can work well in containers, especially when the chosen plant is as beautiful as the diascia. A perennial with terminal clusters of shell-like flowers which have two spurs, it comes in a range of soft pinks. Although rarely grown, it is an undemanding plant and produces a profusion of flowers over a long period in summer, and even into the early autumn. Position it in a sunny spot, where it can be seen to full advantage. It is not that hardy, so only leave outside over winter in gardens that escape the worst of the cold weather.

⚘ Usually the plants that grow into a full, bushy, mounded shape make the best single species arrangements. Among the favourite annuals, pelargoniums, petunias, nasturtiums, and verbena all stand out well on their own, either in one colour or in a glorious, abandoned mixture.

PRACTICAL MATTERS

SOIL
Plant in a well-drained potting mixture of medium nutritional value.
SITE
Place in a sunny position.
WATERING
The potting mixture should be kept moist, but avoid overwatering. Feed once a week.
PLANTS
Grow two diascias in this 27cm- (11in-) diameter, terracotta pot.

Trails of Pink
⚘ The pretty salmon-pink flowers of diascia are borne in profusion along trailing, semi-upright stems in summer and early autumn, almost concealing the terracotta pot from which the plants grow. They should not be allowed to dry out during the summer.

Diascia •
(Diascia rigescens)
This is one of the hardiest species.

STRIKING-LEAVED BEGONIAS

For many years, I had an aversion to begonias; indeed I still find that the very large-flowered, show varieties with day-glo colours are sometimes difficult to live with. Now, I probably over-extol them. Many begonias are subtle in their appeal, and some have very beautiful leaves. The foliage of the rex varieties, used here, comes in a range of subdued, yet exquisite, colours and is often elaborately spotted or striped. They are perennials and are well suited to container culture.

PRACTICAL MATTERS

SOIL
Plant in a rich, well-drained potting mixture.

SITE
Place in a shady site.

WATERING
Water well in the growing and flowering season. Feed once a week.

PLANTS
Plant two rex begonias and four 'Billie Langdon' in a 40cm- (16in-) diameter pot and three 'Norah Bedson' in a 25cm- (10in-) diameter glazed, ceramic pot.

Subdued Scheme
✻ Two deep blue, Chinese glazed pots set off the pure white flowers and highly decorative leaves of these begonias. Plant the tubers of 'Billie Langdon' in spring. The other two varieties are usually grown indoors, but can be placed outdoors in summer.

• Rhizomatous begonia (*Begonia* 'Norah Bedson')
In winter, when the plant is indoors, do not water too much if the light level is low.

• Tuberous begonia (*Begonia* x *tuberhybrida* 'Billie Langdon')
Grown for its plentiful, pure white flowers.

• Rex begonia (*Begonia rex* 'Merry Christmas')
The exotic-looking leaves are evergreen.

SUMMER SHADE LOVERS

ONLY A FEW shade- and semi-shade-loving plants produce masses of beautiful flowers over a long period in summer. Tuberous begonias are some of the showiest. They are not hardy, but you can overwinter them easily. Before the first frosts, take the pots inside and stop watering the plants so they dry off. Remove the browned foliage, gently brush off the soil and store in almost-dry peat, giving them a very small amount of water, occasionally, to stop the tubers shrivelling. Keep in a dry, cool, but frost-free place. Plant the tubers out the following spring.

Here, I have mixed begonias with fuchsias and tobacco plants, also shade lovers. Fuchsias must also be overwintered in a cool but frost-free place. Tobacco plants, short-lived perennials grown as annuals, have the additional advantage of being scented, especially in the evenings.

Tuberous begonia
(*Begonia* x
tuberhybrida)
The large, showy flowers come
in a range of reds, pinks,
oranges,
yellow, and
white.

Intense Colours

✕ Pink, orange, and blood-red begonias, fuchsias, and tobacco plants clash fiercely to create a rich planting for a corner of the garden that receives little sun. Notice how the dark leaves of begonias heighten the glowing effect of the arrangement. The flower display should last from early or mid summer until late autumn.

• **Fuchsia** (*Fuchsia* 'Thalia')
A variety distinguished by its clusters of thin, tubular, bell-like flowers.

Tobacco plant (*Nicotiana alata* Sensation Series)
Lightly scented flowers borne on 60cm- (24in-) high stems.

Pendulous tuberous begonia •
(*Begonia* x *tuberhybrida pendula*)
Trailing begonias, useful for planting at the front of containers.

PRACTICAL MATTERS

•

SOIL

Plant in a well-drained potting mixture of high nutritional value.

SITE

Place in a shady or semi-shady site.

WATERING

Water well and feed weekly during the flowering season.

PLANTS

Grow a mixture of tuberous begonias, tobacco plants, and fuchsias in each 48cm- (19in-) diameter, weathered, terracotta pot, allowing four to five plants per pot.

•

QUARTET OF GLAZED POTS

POTS OF VARYING heights and diameters, each holding just one plant species, can make a most effective arrangement. I tend to choose containers that are strongly linked, either by the material from which they are made, or by the colour of their outer surfaces. Add interest to the group by selecting plants with different growth habits – upright, mounding, trailing or mat-forming – but make sure that they have one common feature to relate them visually.

The containers should also suit the position that you have in mind for them. This group of rich brown, glazed pots would work well if placed on brick or wood, or maybe standing on some informal steps. The glazed terracotta pots seen here are available from most garden centres. Always check whether the pots are frost-hardy. Glazed terracotta pots do not last as long as unglazed pots, so they should be checked for their durability in extreme cold.

Houttuynia *(Houttuynia cordata* 'Chamaeleon')
When crushed, the colourful leaves of this perennial plant give off a pungent, citrus-like smell.

Dwarf aster *(Aster novi-belgii* dwarf form)
An aster bearing masses of rich pink flowers in autumn.

PRACTICAL MATTERS

SOIL
Plant in a potting mixture of high nutritional value.

SITE
All these plants require a sunny position, except houttuynia, which enjoys a little dappled shade.

WATERING
The houttuynia requires moist conditions. For the other plants keep the potting mixture moist, but not soggy. Feed once a week.

PLANTS
One plant is grown in each 23cm- (9in-) diameter pot, with the exception of the asters, when three plants are grown.

Hebe (*Hebe* 'Lindsayi')
One of the hardiest hebes, with
evergreen leaves and a long
flowering season.

Ceratostigma
(*Ceratostigma
plumbaginoides*)
A perennial with flowers
and foliage that both look
their best in late summer
and early autumn.

Autumn Hues

The colours found in the
flowers and foliage of these
autumn plants help unify this
grouping. Notice how the pale
pink spikes of the hebe and the
richer hues of the dwarf asters
pick out the splashes of colour
found in the houttuynia's foliage.
While the ceratostigma produces
its intense blue flowers in autumn,
its leaves also turn a rich red,
reflecting the other warm hues
around them. Glazed clay pots are
ideal for setting off the autumn
flower and foliage colours.

DECORATIVE BERRIES

FEW PLANTS PRODUCE such a dramatic range of coloured berries as pernettya and its hybrids. Set off by the small, glossy, evergreen leaves, the fruits vary from dark plum-red, through bright red, to pink, and finally white. Only the female plants carry berries, although it is necessary to have a male plant nearby for pollination. In this arrangement, a male shrub has been introduced among the more decorative females, but you could grow one in a nearby border. As pernettya is evergreen and hardy, you could keep it in this glazed, ceramic pot permanently to enjoy its glossy foliage in winter, and then its tiny white flowers in the spring and early summer.

PRACTICAL MATTERS

SOIL
Plant in a slightly acid potting mixture.

SITE
Place in a sunny site.

WATERING
Keep the soil moist through the growing season. Feed once a fortnight.

PLANTS
Grow four pernettyas in a 40cm- (16in-) diameter, glazed, ceramic pot.

Pernettya (*Pernettya mucronata* 'Edward Ball')
A male plant.

Pernettya (*Pernettya mucronata* 'Bell's Seedling')
A female plant bearing bright red fruits.

Pernettya (*Pernettya mucronata* 'Mulberry Wine')
A female plant that bears dusky pink fruits.

Pernettya (*Pernettya mucronata alba*)
A female variety grown for its white fruits.

Green Harmony
This large, rich green, glazed and frost-proofed pot has a strong affinity with the colour of the pernettyas' small, spiky leaves, yet at the same time it provides a perfect foil for the shining, red, white, and pink berries that appear in the autumn.

CHRYSANTHEMUM TREE

With their strong resemblance to miniature trees, plants grown as standards look most attractive in terracotta pots.

✶ The best plants to train into flowering, mop-headed standards are spray chrysanthemums, fuchsias, and pelargoniums. Take cuttings in autumn and overwinter them under glass. Remove side shoots as the plant grows, and support the main stem with a cane, approximately 1m (36in) long. When the main stem reaches 75cm (30in) high, leave the side shoots to grow; when the stem reaches 1m (36in), pinch out the growing tip, then allow the side shoots to bush out.

✶ Evergreen shrubs can also be trained in this way, but they are slower growing: a standard box or bay tree might take four years to develop a 1m- (36in-) high stem. Although lacking in significant flowers, all make elegant, evergreen displays when clipped to shape.

Chrysanthemum
(*Chrysanthemum* 'Dawn Mist')
A perennial, bearing sprays of single, white, daisy-like flowers tinged pink.

Stonecrop (*Sedum sieboldii* 'Folius medio-variegatus')
A trailing succulent that has tiny, pink, star-like flowers in mid autumn.

Flowering Standard
✶ The colouring in the blooms of this standard chrysanthemum is echoed by the foliage and flowers of stonecrop that grow around its stem.

PRACTICAL MATTERS

SOIL
Plant in a loam-based potting mixture of medium nutritional value.

SITE
Overwinter in a light, frost-free situation, then move to a sunny position in late spring when danger of frost has passed.

WATERING
Avoid overwatering. Feed once a week.

PLANTS
Grow one standard chrysanthemum and six stonecrops in a 40cm- (16in-) diameter, terracotta pot.

Low Bowls

Low bowls are comfortable-looking containers for plants. Unpretentious, and often hardly visible below the planting, they should carry a mound of plants just a little above the ground. They are at their most attractive when they can be seen from above, or at least from a fairly high angle. If the bowl is very shallow, there will be only a little room for the roots, limiting the type of plants you can grow. In very shallow bowls, only succulents, such as houseleeks, will grow well. If you want to grow low annuals and trailing perennials, use bowls that are at least 15cm (6in) deep.

KITCHENWARE

Many containers used in the home can easily become low bowls in the garden, although if they started life as watertight vessels you will need to drill holes in them to provide adequate drainage. Bowls made of glazed ceramic are easily damaged by frost, so save them for summer and early autumn plantings, and use hardier containers for year-round displays.

❦ Antique coppers (old-fashioned washing pots) and copper milk or cream pans are not easy to find, but they make the most beautiful plant containers. You can leave them outside over winter, and, as they weather, the copper becomes oxidized and changes to a wonderful greeny blue hue. This weathering process can be hurried along by painting the outside surface of the vessel either with vinegar or some cheap wine.

MIX AND MATCH

A group of bowls can make a simple but effective display at the base of a flower bed, provided the plants behind them are not too tall. Plants that make hummocky shapes, or those that are trailers,

LAVENDER HUES
Blue marguerites, pansies, pale blue lobelia, and convolvulus (ABOVE) combine in a planting scheme intended to complement the lavender backdrop.

COPPER COLOURING
An antique, copper cream bowl (LEFT) is planted with marigolds and cigar flowers, which were chosen to reflect the colour of the container and the brick paviours.

tend to look best in low bowls. Echo colours found in the flower bed in the arrangements for the bowls. I like to see very simple plantings in bowls – perhaps a planting of one type of ivy, sweet alyssum, or lobelia. You could also try pendulous begonias, pansies, pinks, or bellflowers.

❦ If you want to mix plants, I find that the bowl should be more than 30cm (12in) across, but even then, I think it is best to restrict the colour range. If you want to introduce more than one colour, use more than one bowl, but still stick to colours that relate to each other and plants that have similar forms.

SEASONAL SCHEMES

In a sunny or semi-shady position during the summer, a bowl of cranesbill (*Geranium endressii*), with its non-stop display of pretty, little, pink flowers, a bowl of lilac-coloured pansies, and a larger bowl of Californian bluebells are breath-taking. On shady paving, against a backdrop of green foliage, you could grow bowls of the yellow-flowering, gold-leaved, creeping Jenny, cranesbill (*Geranium nodosum*), with its delicate, cup-shaped pink flowers, and the pick-a-back plant.

❦ For spring in semi-shade or shade, try planting bowls of miniature tulips, maybe one bowl of red 'Plaisir', one of creamy white 'Concerto', and another one of 'Toronto' with its bright red flowers, brown-yellow base, and bronze anthers.

❦ In winter, bowls of different ivies look effective standing on a garden table or arranged in a line along the top of a low wall. The golden-variegated forms, and the yellow-leaved variety, 'Buttercup', are especially attractive, introducing some light relief among the dark, glossy evergreens, which tend to dominate a garden during the colourless, cold, winter months.

FLOWERING BERGENIAS

BERGENIAS ARE HANDSOME AND HARDY, low, evergreen perennials with large leaves that look attractive at a sparse time of the year – in the depths of winter. During mild spells they may flower in mid winter, although the main display is from late winter to early spring. They are extremely easy to grow, requiring little attention apart from judicious watering. Leucothöes have beautiful, evergreen foliage that is often green, but sometimes tinged red in winter.

PRACTICAL MATTERS

SOIL
Plant in well-drained, acid potting mixture.

SITE
A sheltered, semi-shady position is best.

WATERING
Keep well watered. Remember that the large leaves form a barrier to rain.

PLANTS
Grow three bergenias and two leucothöe in a 42cm- (17in-) diameter, reconstituted stone bowl.

Leucothöe
(*Leucothöe* 'Scarletta')
In autumn and winter the leaves are bronze coloured.

Bergenia (*Bergenia* 'Ballawley')
The large leaves turn deep red in autumn, and spires of rich pink flowers appear in winter and spring.

Perfect Timing
❧ Bergenias are at their best towards the end of winter; the new leaves emerge, rich pink flowers form, and last year's old, deep red foliage remains. Here, they grow beside a variety of leucothöe with glossy green leaves tinged an attractive bronze.

SPRING BLUES

BLUE AND WHITE is a beautiful spring colour combination: clean and fresh, it is a scheme that echoes the intense blue skies of early spring. It seemed appropriate to plant this arrangement of grape hyacinths, periwinkle, and Siberian squill in a blue, ceramic bowl. Grape hyacinths have a delicious scent, which is sweet and buttery. If taken indoors, they fill an entire room with their fragrance. The grape hyacinths are posed behind a trailing lesser periwinkle, which is covered with flowers in late winter and early spring. To the right, a clump of Siberian squill, another small, spring bulb, grows.

PRACTICAL MATTERS

SOIL
Plant in a well-drained, lightweight potting mixture of medium nutritional value.

SITE
Ideally set in semi shade.

WATERING
Through the winter, keep the potting mixture just moist.

PLANTS
Grow one periwinkle, twenty-five grape hyacinth bulbs, and ten Siberian squill in a 45cm- (18in-) diameter, frost-proof, ceramic bowl.

Grape hyacinth
(Muscari azureum)
A variety producing sky-blue, scented flowers.

Grape hyacinth
(Muscari botryoides 'Album')
A white-flowered variety.

Close-at-hand
✗ Set this bowl of blue and white spring flowers on a garden table close to the house, so it can easily be seen, and frequently visited for a quick whiff of the grape hyacinth's delicious, sweet butter scent.

Variegated foliage
A lesser periwinkle with variegated leaves is also available. Perhaps grow it with white grape hyacinths instead of the blue variety.

Lesser periwinkle
(Vinca minor)
An evergreen perennial that spreads rapidly and produces a succession of flowers over a long period.

Siberian squill
(Scilla siberica)
Delicate, clear blue, bell-like flowers appear on short stems after the leaves have emerged.

CHINESE BOWL OF SUN ROSES

As mid summer approaches, it is difficult to keep up with the profusion of flowers in the garden. While most of the flowering plants can be grown in the larger containers, only those with a shallow root run – annuals and some low-growing shrubs – are suitable for planting in bowls. Halimiocistus, an evergreen shrub producing silky, saucer-shaped flowers for many weeks in summer, has been chosen for this glazed, Chinese bowl. To perform well, it needs sun and a very well-drained soil, as it hates to be soggy at the roots. It will not tolerate too much frost, especially when combined with damp conditions.

Other summer-flowering shrubs that do well in low bowls include rock roses, fuchsias, convolvulus, heathers, hebes, lavender, and potentillas.

Bowls filled with plants that have outward-facing or pendulous flowers, such as fuchsias and ceanothus, are most effectively displayed above ground level, perhaps on a low wall or garden table. Those with flowers that face upwards – rock roses, potentillas, and convolvulus – are best on the ground.

PRACTICAL MATTERS

SOIL
Plant in a very well-drained potting mixture of medium nutritional value, and gravel (proportions 4:1).

SITE
Place in a sunny site. In cold areas, provide frost and wind protection.

WATERING
Do not overwater or allow the roots to become soggy. Feed once a fortnight.

PLANTS
Grow three halimiocistus in a 38cm-(15in-) long, oval, glazed, ceramic bowl.

• **Halimiocistus** (x *Halimiocistus wintonensis* 'Merrist Wood Cream') An evergreen shrub that reaches 60cm (24in) high and flowers in early and mid summer.

Colour Co-ordination

✿ Often a container will
suggest the plants that look
best in it. Notice, here, how
the yellow flowers and grey-
green foliage of halimiocistus
subtly echo the mustard and
ochre colouring of the glazed,
ceramic, Chinese bowl.

PINK AND MAUVE TRIO

WITH A FEW EXCEPTIONS, summer annuals do not tend to grow very tall, and so make ideal subjects for low bowls, especially the plants that sprawl or form a dome. I have used semi-shade-loving busy Lizzies in several plantings because they are versatile, they have a very long flowering period, attractive leaves, and an ease of growth that is matched by few other plants. They will grow in any situation, even strong sun, although they then will need extra water to compensate for the drying effect of such conditions. If there is any problem, it is that they tend to take over in a mixed planting, so you have to cut them back as soon as they start to overpower smaller plants, such as the floss flowers used here.

A wealth of other annuals would be just as successful in this bowl. Among the sun lovers, there are pelargoniums – either upright or trailing ivy-leaved varieties – low-growing dahlias, petunias, lobelias, snapdragons, chrysanthemums, sweet alyssum, marigolds, verbenas, and nasturtiums. For low bowls in semi-shade or shade, try begonias (which are as versatile as busy Lizzies), low-growing tobacco plants, any of a multitude of fuchsias, and pansies.

Verbena (*Verbena tenera* 'Mahonettii') Sadly, this pretty variety has no scent.

Floss flower (*Ageratum* 'Bengali') The small, delicate flowers contrast with the bolder blossoms of the busy Lizzie.

PRACTICAL MATTERS

SOIL
Plant in a well-drained, rich potting mixture.

SITE
Place in a semi-shady site.

WATERING
Keep just moist and feed once a week.

PLANTS
Grow four busy Lizzies, three floss flowers, and three verbena in a 42cm- (17in-) diameter, terracotta bowl.

Florists' Begonias

✄ The begonias in this fluted bowl can be bought in a flower shop. In summer, they thrive outside in a bright but shady place, and will produce masses of flowers. They are prone to mildew attacks, and slugs and snails may be a problem.

• **Busy Lizzy** (*Impatiens* New Guinea hybrid) Produces a mass of flowers and beautifully coloured foliage.

Busy Lizzy Bowl

✄ A large, ribbed terracotta bowl with a pink colour scheme, based on New Guinea busy Lizzies with variegated leaves, pink floss flowers, and a little, twinkly verbena. In a semi-shady or sunny position, this arrangement will flower from early summer until the first frosts.

URNS AND JARS

URNS ARE THE MOST BEAUTIFUL of all containers. By definition, they can be any large jar or vessel that is rounded in shape, but they are usually grand containers with open, flaring or bulbous top sections, balanced on feet or base columns. Originally, they were made to hold the ashes of the dead, and they had a lid: the word urn comes from the Latin *urere*, meaning to burn, and the Greek for a jar, *hurhke*.

— GARDEN ORNAMENTS —

Urns have been used as garden ornaments for centuries. They became especially popular in seventeenth- and eighteenth-century Italy. Made from stone, lead, or terracotta, they were often extremely decorative with swagging, fluting and elaborate, carved handles. The Victorians produced quantities of urns: many of the cast iron ones can still be found, but for a high, often extortionate, price.

⚜ It has to be said that antique urns sometimes look best used like a piece of sculpture, as an unplanted garden ornament. The many reproductions of classical urns made in reconstituted stone and fibreglass as well as terracotta, however, are better planted up.

⚜ Although most urns tend to be tall compared with their base section, they do not look good holding tall plants. This is especially true of the classical type of urn, with a bulbous top and narrowing stem flaring down to a square base, which sits on a short or tall column that is either cylindrical or straight edged. These urns tend to look best when their planting approximately reflects the height of the container part of the urn, and has a good mass of sideways growth. Since

ANTIQUE URN
Pink-flowering diascia and the delicate, silver-leaved plecostachys brim over the edges of a magnificent lead urn (ABOVE), strategically placed to the side of a gravel path.

BORDER SITUATION
A terracotta urn filled with yellow daisies and black-eyed Susan (LEFT) stands discreetly in a mixed border, adding height and colour in mid summer.

the urn is already on a stem, a plant with an exposed trunk looks uncomfortable. Choose plants that make a fountain shape, appearing to emanate from the centre of the urn's base.

— STRATEGIC SITING —

Like very large pots and troughs, urns can be extremely weighty, and it is impractical to move them around too often. So think about the site carefully. Place them in important positions on your best lines of sight, maybe on an axis leading from a major house window, or at the end of a long path. A pair of small urns looks good on either side of a path as it leaves a terrace, or flanking a flight of steps; a single urn is exciting at the crossing of two paths, especially if there is a vista leading to it. Otherwise, urns can be placed against tall walls or dark green hedges, and beside any doorways and arches. Positioning an urn informally in a border is a beautiful way of bringing interest to an area that lacks colour at a particular time of year. Urns can also look splendid planted in the centre of a formal pond. If access is difficult, plant them with something like ivy, perhaps, that requires only minimum attention.

— EXOTIC OIL JARS —

Oil jars from the Mediterranean or large Chinese jars also make stunning containers, although you will need to drill drainage holes. Also, find out if they will stand your climate. The Greek and part-glazed jars from the south of France are barely frost-proof. They all look best with a profusion of trailing plants tumbling out of them. Without drainage holes, you can fill them with water to reflect the sky, or grow delicate, small-leaved aquatic plants in them.

FOUNTAIN OF FLOWERS

GETTING THE PROPORTIONS for plantings in urns right is not easy. Surprisingly, tall plants often appear most uncomfortable, whereas low plantings work better. A simple arrangement, such as a single planting of ivy, can look wonderful spilling over the lip of an urn like flowing water. This well-proportioned stone urn is magnificent filled with plants that spray out of it like a fountain. The broom makes a great show in late spring, but its roots soon leave little room for the addition of other plants. If you want colour in the summer, transplant the broom after it has flowered and replace it with summer annuals.

Broom (*Cytisus* 'Cornish Cream')
In late spring, the slender stems are wreathed with scented flowers.

Peony-flowered tulip
(*Tulipa* 'Carnival de Nice')
The striped, double globular flowers are produced late in the season.

Spring Urn
Cream and yellow, with touches of red, make a cheerful combination for late spring. Plant the ivy, broom, and tulip bulbs in late autumn. As the broom has very delicate stems and foliage, it does not impede the tulips' growth.

Ivy (*Hedera helix* 'Telecurl')
Plant ivy around the edge, to soften the sides without concealing its graceful outline.

PRACTICAL MATTERS

SOIL
Plant in a potting mixture of medium nutritional value.

SITE
Place in a sunny site.

WATERING
Keep the potting mixture moist, but not soggy.

PLANTS
Grow two broom, ten tulip bulbs, and five ivies in a stone urn, the bowl of which measures 42cm (17in) across and 35cm (14in) deep.

CHINESE JAR

Lantana (*Lantana camara*)
Varieties range from red and pink through orange, yellow, and white.

Golden feverfew (*Chrysanthemum parthenium* 'Aureum')
The delicate leaves and flowers have an astringent aroma.

Plectranthus (*Plectranthus coleoides* 'Variegatus')
A foliage plant that is ideal for containers.

Plecostachys (*Plecostachys serpyllifolia*)
The tiny, silver leaves tumble over the sides of the jar.

Chinese jars or urns make fabulous containers. I felt the colours of this jar called for a yellow and cream planting. Lantana is a good choice as it is a quick-growing annual that is covered in flowers all summer. Feverfew, with its froth of white flowers and delicate leaves, seeds itself all over my garden, so I often use it in my summer container plantings. The silver, trailing plecostachys and variegated plectranthus complete the picture. All but the feverfew are tender, so bring the arrangement in for winter.

SOIL
Plant in a potting mixture of medium to rich nutritional value.
SITE
Place in a sunny site.
WATERING
Water well in hot, sunny weather. Feed once a fortnight.
PLANTS
Grow one lantana, two plectranthus, four plecostachys, and two golden feverfew in a Chinese jar, 45cm (18in) across and 52cm (21in) deep.

Tall Order
✕ Rising from a mass of bushy and trailing, variegated and silver-leaved plants, the tall lantana complements the shape of the Chinese jar. Remove any lantana seedheads to encourage more flowers.

STATELY SPLENDOUR

WIDE URNS LOOK THEIR BEST when filled by plants with a spreading habit. The curving shape of the base of this urn suggests that the plants also should have an outward-curving form. The bowl of the urn is quite shallow and larger plants would not grow happily in it, which is just as well as they would look uncomfortable.

※ If a wide urn is placed on a wall or high column, so that it is primarily seen from below, it is best planted with trailers such as evergreen ivies, periwinkles, or flowering, ivy-leaved pelargoniums, petunias, fuchsias, or pendulous begonias.

—— A REFRESHING CHANGE ——

It is always fun to have a change from the old faithfuls, so here I have created an arrangement with pentas, lantana, and the prostrate weigela 'Looymansii Aurea'. Pale pink, orange, and pale yellow with lime-green makes a stylish combination. The planting will be in flower for many weeks, and then will have attractive foliage from spring through the summer. Pentas and lantana are tender, and therefore need to be grown as annuals in colder areas, but the gold-leaved weigela is hardy.

※ Another interesting arrangement for this urn could be an all-white display, which always looks elegant. You could use 'Mont Blanc' lavatera, the variegated, ivy-leaved pelargonium, 'Elegante', and 'Daybreak' gazanias. In spring, try a mass planting of 'Greuze' tulips, or one of the scented narcissi, and surround it with 'La Grave' periwinkle.

PRACTICAL MATTERS
•
SOIL
Plant in a well-drained, rich potting mixture.
SITE
Place in a site that has sun for part of the day.
WATERING
Keep well watered and feed every two weeks.
PLANTS
Grow five lantana, three pentas, and three weigela in a 75cm- (30in-) diameter, reconstituted stone urn.
•

Soft-coloured Stone
※ A soft, sand-coloured, reconstituted stone urn with a summer planting of some lesser-known species: lantana, pentas, and a gold-leaved weigela. Planted to be seen from almost any angle, it would look good standing on a square stone column at the end of a straight path, or on a wall stanchion or pillar on a terrace.

Pentas (*Pentas lanceolata*)
Produces clusters of pink,
lilac, red, or white flowers
in summer and autumn.

Lantana (*Lantana camara*)
Pinch out the tips of young
lantana plants to promote a
full, bushy habit.

Weigela (*Weigela*
'Looymansii Aurea')
To maintain vigour, prune out
a few old branches to ground
level after flowering.

BARRELS AND TUBS

IN SOME INSTANCES, you may find that you require an especially big container – perhaps to grow shrubs, small trees, or simply a large planting. Garden centres now have a wide range on sale, including ceramic and terracotta tubs, fibreglass planters, and old beer barrels. There is also scope for improvisation. Bread crocks and various other vessels from the kitchen can be used as containers for growing plants, if you drill holes in the base.

FIBREGLASS

As fibreglass can easily be moulded to any shape, and coloured in any shade, it is widely used to make simple plant tubs or replicas of wooden Versailles planters, elaborate lead vessels, and other antique containers that are hard to find and extremely expensive. If done well, fibreglass imitations can look most convincing. They are moderately hard wearing, they are light to move around, and they require little maintenance.

BEER BARRELS

Originally, the familiar wooden barrel with iron bands was used for maturing and storing beer. Cut in half, it makes an excellent container for plants, and will last outside for several years, until the metal bands rust away. It is important to keep the wood of this type of barrel moist; if allowed to dry out, the wood contracts, the metal bands fall off, and the barrel collapses. Usually, moisture from the soil is adequate to prevent this from happening. It is always worth checking barrels bought from garden centres because if they have been stored empty for some time, the wood may have dried out. If this

RHODODENDRONS ON STEPS
Half barrels (ABOVE) are planted with pink and purple rhododendrons, to complement the spectacular backdrop of irises.

QUEEN OF THE NIGHT
A plain, wooden, half barrel (LEFT) filled with the beautiful, almost black tulip 'Queen of Night' looks dramatic against the lime green bracts of spurge.

is the case, give the barrel a thorough soaking before you plant it up. If you get barrels from a brewery, you may have to drill some 1cm- ($\frac{1}{2}$in-) drainage holes, in the base.

To help preserve the wood of barrels, you can prime and paint them. Choose a colour that suits the barrel's intended site. Whilst white, black, and green fit most situations, the more adventurous colours can work well if they pick up the paint on the exterior woodwork of the house, or enhance the plantings. Yellow sets off golden-leaved plants, and grey goes well with silver foliage.

PLANT CHOICE

Because of their size, tubs and barrels are especially useful for growing shrubs and small trees with large root runs. Spring bulbs, especially the taller growing narcissi and tulips, look effective too, their bare upright stems echoing the straight sides of a tub. I like using just one species or variety. A group of a single variety of ivy plants looks particularly well, covering and tumbling over a large barrel, and will maintain interest all through the year. In summer, a mass of petunias or low-growing roses look magnificent.

WATER GARDEN

If the barrel or tub is watertight, you can fill it with water and grow some aquatic plants, perhaps miniature water lilies and some small floating species (SEE PAGE 112). Make sure that you support the water-lily roots at exactly the correct depth below the water surface. If necessary, prop up the basket in which the roots are held with a couple of bricks. Keep the surface of the water clean, and top up with water whenever it is necessary.

BLUE CONIFER

GIVEN THE CORRECT SOIL CONDITIONS, good drainage, and enough water to prevent them from becoming very dry, most conifers grow well in containers. Lack of water is the most frequent cause of dying back so you must check the potting mixture's moisture content throughout the winter, as well as the rest of the year. Remember, though, never to water plants in freezing conditions.

🖾 Many conifers, especially pines, spruces, and junipers, tolerate exposed positions. The low-growing species make attractive and long-lived specimens and have interestingly coloured foliage, ranging through the brightest lime-greens to intense silver-blues. Of the larger and faster-growing conifers, *Picea* 'Albertiana Conica' makes a wonderful specimen tree in a big container; forming a vivid green, closely packed pyramid – keep it out of strong winds or it will become scorched. *Pinus mugo* and *Pinus wallichiana* are other striking specimen trees. They also form an excellent windbreak for an exposed site.

PRACTICAL MATTERS

SOIL
Plant in a neutral or acid potting mixture with sharp sand added (proportions 5:1).
SITE
Place in a sunny or exposed site.
WATERING
Keep the potting mixture moist.
PLANTS
Grow two spruce and four ivies in a 48cm- (19in-) diameter, frost-proof, ceramic tub.

❧ PLANTING A CONIFER ❧

1 *Place a layer of clean crocks in the base of a frost-proof, ceramic tub and firm in lime-free potting mixture mixed with sharp sand, to the base of the plants' root level.*

2 *Soak the root balls of two flat-sided blue spruce for about one hour in a bucket of water, and then position them in the tub so that they sit comfortably together. Firm the soil around their root balls, and fill the tub, planting the ivies around the edge.*

3 *Make sure that the soil is well firmed all around the arrangement and water it well. Blue spruce grows slowly so you need only prune the occasional, stray shoot growing in the wrong direction to keep the shrubs in a neat shape. Do not allow the potting mixture to become too dry or too wet.*

Silver Spring Leaves
🖾 Three years later, this arrangement has grown so much that it is ready for repotting – late spring is a good time for planting and repotting conifers and most other evergreen shrubs. Seen here in mid spring, the new shoots are about to burst into foliage that is an even more intense silver than the old leaves.

• **Blue spruce** (*Picea pungens* 'Glauca')
Conifers grow well in containers as they do not require long root runs.

• **Ivy** (*Hedera helix* 'Sagittifolia Variegata')
Variegated and deeply lobed leaves add contrast to this permanent evergreen planting.

VINE BARREL

IERIS IS ONE OF THOSE INVALUABLE SHRUBS that looks attractive throughout the year, and therefore makes an excellent basis for a permanent planting in a container. Its glossy, evergreen foliage forms a marvellous backdrop for the more seasonal flowering plants, although it also has spectacular, seasonal displays of its own. In spring, for example, the new leaves that unfurl are brilliant pink, before fading to pale pink and then bright yellow-green. At the same time, sprays of white flowers, reminiscent of lily-of-the-valley, come out. In this mid spring arrangement, cineraria have been planted among the pieris: their vibrant heads of daisy-like flowers form a striking association with the new, pink pieris leaves. Cineraria are usually grown as house plants, but they do extremely well outside in a frost-free spot, if you plant them just as their flowers open.

—— YEAR-ROUND SHOW ——

In early spring, before the cineraria are ready, plant pockets of narcissi between the pieris. They will look stunning alongside its evergreen leaves. In summer, fill the gaps with annuals: tobacco plants, large-growing New Guinea hybrid busy Lizzies, or fuchsias. Like the pieris, all these plants enjoy shade or semi-shade; they also grow happily in the acidic potting mixture required by the pieris.

When there is no seasonal planting in the barrel, and the pieris are growing alone, leave pots filled with soil in the position reserved for seasonal plantings. This will prevent the shrubs' roots from invading the spaces and allow you to easily put new plants in the spaces.

PRACTICAL MATTERS

SOIL
Plant in a well-drained, acid potting mixture of high nutritional value.

SITE
Place in a semi-shady position, sheltered from wind, and protected from frost.

WATERING
Keep well watered, but not saturated, and feed once a fortnight from spring until autumn.

PLANTS
Grow three pieris, four cinerarias, and five ivies in a wooden vine barrel.

Light padding
As the vine barrel is very tall, I have padded out its base with a 25cm- (10in-) layer of broken polystyrene. This acts as a drainage medium and also prevents the container from becoming too heavy.

Relic from a Vineyard

✄ This antique vine barrel is planted up with variegated pieris and floriferous cinerarias. The wine barrel comes from a French vineyard where it was used to carry grapes from the fields to the press. If planting up a similar barrel, ensure that it has adequate drainage holes. Do not let the wood dry out too much, or it will shrink, loosening the iron bands that hold it together.

Pieris (*Pieris* 'Flaming Silver')
A pretty, variegated form with pink new shoots in spring.

Cineraria (*Senecio* x *hybridus*)
The flowers are so profuse in late winter, spring, and early summer that they conceal the evergreen leaves.

Ivy (*Hedera helix* 'Pittsburgh')
A plain green ivy that does extremely well in containers.

Quick Change-over

✄ If you leave the cinerarias in their individual pots in the container, they are easier to remove when the flowers are over. This means that you must water them frequently to prevent the soil from drying out. Once the cinerarias are over, replace them with summer-flowering annuals.

BARREL OF PETUNIAS

M OST PETUNIAS ARE HALF-HARDY PERENNIALS but they are best grown as annuals, as the plants tend to become leggy and less floriferous in their second year. In their first year, they flower continuously from early summer until autumn, but as with most plants that flower for a very long season, it is important to deadhead spent blooms to keep the display going. Their leaves and stems are covered with downy hairs and the leaves are also quite sticky, so grow them away from heavy pollution or they will gradually become smothered in black dust.

Petunias have been extensively hybridized and the variety of colours and flower forms now available is enormous. Colours range from deep, velvety purple through violet, red, pink, and yellow, to white. Some have striped and splashed petals, and others sport a band of contrasting colour around the edge of each flower. Some flowers are small, some large, some single, some double, and a few have a rich, sweet scent that is almost as heady as gardenia. The larger-flowered varieties are liable to spot in rain, but the smaller-flowered Resisto hybrids are more weather-resistant.

PRACTICAL MATTERS

SOIL
Plant in a well-drained potting mixture of low nutritional value.

SITE
Place in a warm, sunny site.

WATERING
Keep well watered but not soggy and feed only occasionally to promote flowers rather than leaves.

PLANTS
Grow 24 petunias in a 90cm- (36in-) diameter, half, wooden beer barrel.

• Petunia
(*Petunia* x *hybrida*).
A selection of petunias,
imaginatively chosen for
their colours.

Colour Permutations

This colour mix of ice-pink, corn-yellow,
and deep pink with a cream eye, relates
well to the old, half beer barrel. A
selection of striped varieties, pale blue,
cream, and white flowers, or maybe
brightly mixed doubles, would also make
an attractive combination. Light and dark,
rich reds look jazzy together, too.

CROCK OF ROSES

IF YOU LOVE ROSES and want to grow some in containers, the smaller-growing multifloras, miniatures, and patio roses are the ones to choose. Their compact habit, tiny leaves, and small but full blossoms are neater than the larger-growing roses, so their shape looks comfortable in containers. You can try the larger-growing roses in pots, but, as they need a deep root run, they tend not to produce as many flowers as they would in the open ground. Since they are

not the most beautiful plants, they can look ungainly for long periods, but you may feel that their spectacular blooms make up for this.

❦ Miniature roses and the new patio roses (crosses between miniatures and floribundas that have been specifically developed for containers) are being bred all the time, giving you many varieties from which to choose. I always try to select ones that smell sweet, such as 'Robin Redbreast', a cheerful variety with bright scarlet flowers with pale eyes. 'Stars 'n' Stripes' is another favourite, bred from the old rose 'Ferdinand Pichard'. It has white flowers splashed with purple and crimson, and a wonderful, old rose scent.

Rose (*Rosa* 'Robin Redbreast') A patio rose that has been specially developed for growing in containers.

Second Life

❦ A broken lid ended this bread crock's useful life in the kitchen. By boring two 1cm (³/₈in) holes in the base with a masonry drill, I easily transformed it into a plant container. As the roses are low-growing, the tall crock lifts them up from the ground, making it easy to smell them as you walk past.

PRACTICAL MATTERS

•

SOIL
Plant in a rich, well-drained potting mixture.

SITE
Place in a sunny site or one that receives sun for half of the day.

WATERING
Water well but do not allow to become soggy. Feed once a week.

PLANTS
Grow three 'Robin Redbreast' roses in a 35cm- (14in-) diameter, bread crock.

•

SUMMER SALAD

THERE IS SOMETHING SPECIAL about picking your own fruit, vegetables, and herbs. While it is quite easy to grow most herbs in containers, fewer fruits and vegetables do sufficiently well in containers to warrant growing them in this way. Tomatoes are the most successful, cropping heavily when grown in a rich potting mixture and fed and watered well. Courgettes grown under the same conditions also crop well. You can plant them in succession to produce fruits from mid summer until autumn. Strawberries and blueberries are other fruits that also have good yields when grown in containers.

PRACTICAL MATTERS

SOIL
Plant in a very rich, well-drained potting mixture.

SITE
Place in a sunny site.

WATERING
Water well during the growing season and feed with tomato fertilizer two to three times a week.

PLANTS
Grow three tomato plants and two courgette plants in a 72cm- (30in-) square, fibreglass tub.

Tomato (*Lycopersicon lycopersicum* 'Red Ensign') A healthy grower that sets fruit early. Train up stakes, removing side shoots and stopping at six hands, and syringe flowers to help set fruit.

Courgette (*Cucurbita pepo* 'Zucchini') An excellent cropper with thin skins.

Garden Produce
✕ Tomatoes and courgettes grow well in a large, fibreglass tub in a sunny site. As the leaves of tomato plants begin to yellow when the fruit ripens, this is not the most aesthetic planting in late summer, so choose a discreet site for it in your garden.

SINKS AND TROUGHS

THE IDEA of planting a sink or a trough with garden plants is relatively new, but they both make marvellous containers. Sinks and troughs have been used in utilitarian ways for centuries, either in kitchens and sculleries, or on farms. The early ones were made from stone, and have the advantage of almost looking as if they are part of the landscape. The more recent sinks are usually made of porcelain.

✠ If you are lucky enough to have a stone sink, then prize it and give it a prominent place in your garden. Either set it on the ground or raise it up on legs made from stones or bricks.

— WEIGHT PROBLEM —

The one drawback of a stone sink is that it is very heavy. I have one that weighs substantially more than a grand piano, according to my furniture removers, but it is possible to move it on the level, solo, using a lever, and broom handles as rollers. Levering up the trough, position three broom handles at regular intervals underneath it, to act as rollers. Slowly push the trough forward, and as each roller is freed at the back, take it around to the front and position it to take the weight of the trough as it rolls forward again. It is a slow, but relatively effortless, process.

— CONTEMPORARY ALTERNATIVES —

Porcelain sinks are not as heavy as their stone counterparts, but if you cover them with a stone mix (SEE PAGES 158-9), they become almost as weighty. A range of troughs specifically for garden use is now available in lighter materials. The wooden ones are very attractive, but check that the wood will last. Teak or cedar troughs are the best – and the most expensive. To prolong the wood's life, paint the inside of the trough with a wood preservative and also line the trough with strong polythene, making holes to coincide with the drainage holes in the base.

✠ Some of the fibreglass troughs are made to simulate lead or wood panels and can look quite convincing, especially when you leave them outside for a year or so to weather.

— LOW PLANTINGS —

As sinks and troughs are relatively low in comparison with their width, it seems natural to plant them with low plants: sinks tend to look out of proportion when they have plants that are on the tall side. In a sunny site, plants, such as alpines, that normally grow in rocky or stony places, are a good choice for sinks or troughs. They are also suitable for exposed sites as most alpines tolerate wind, cold, and harsh sun. Make a miniature rock garden, carefully placing a group of small rocks on the surface of the potting mixture (SEE PAGES 158-9). In a shady site, sinks and troughs look beautiful when decorated with old pieces of rugged tree bark and planted with small ferns. A stone sink also makes a good home for a collection of houseleeks or small, silver-leaved succulents.

✠ All alpines must be protected from winter wet, otherwise they will rot and die. In sheltered spots, you can do this by driving a small stick into each corner of your sink and balancing a pane of glass on top. The glass must not touch the plants, so leave a 15cm (6in) gap between them and the glass. It is essential to have plenty of ventilation. Alternatively, you can secure an open-ended cloche over small sinks, driving it in with stakes.

LEAD HEIRLOOM
A handsome, eighteenth-century lead trough (ABOVE), planted with petunias, purple sage, pansies, marguerites, helichrysum, scented pelargoniums, and an abutilon, is set against the plain background of an evergreen hedge.

SINK GARDEN
A selection of succulents and alpines (LEFT), growing in various stone sinks and a terracotta roof tile on a hot, sunny terrace. Each sink is raised slightly off the ground to ensure that water can drain out of the plug holes freely.

WOODLAND GARDEN

IF YOU ARE FORTUNATE ENOUGH to have a large, old stone sink, but it is in a fairly shady place, do not feel that you have to struggle to move it to a sunnier spot in your garden. A good selection of very beautiful plants with wonderful shapes, colours, and perfumes will grow happily without that much sun.

✗ These semi-shade-loving spring bulbs and flowers growing on a bed of moss make a tranquil, enchanting, semi-wild planting that is reminiscent of a woodland floor. Dog's tooth violets are one of my great favourites with their flowers of white, cream, or pink with waxy, reflexed petals. So, too, are the snake's head fritillaries. When seen close at hand, their papery, pendent flowers resemble the finest china with an elaborate pattern of veining, varying from almost white, through pink to purple and plum-black.

✗ Sadly, cowslips are not as prevalent in the wild as they used to be even though they are now a protected species, but they are easy to grow from seed and have a delicious, sweet, buttery scent. Lily-of-the-valley have one of the best scents of all but they are unpredictable. Either they grow like a rampant weed, or they are impossible to start – I know people who have struggled for years to get them established without success. If you find that you cannot persuade lily-of-the-valley to grow in your garden, try uvularia, another shade lover, instead.

Natural Colonizers

✗ All the plants in this stone sink will naturalise, forming larger clumps each year, which can be divided. As the dog's tooth violets and snake's head fritillaries die down after flowering, introduce small summer and autumn interest plants over the top of the bulbs and beside them.

Lithodora
(*Lithodora diffusa* 'Heavenly Blue')
Flowers over a long period.

Lily-of-the-valley
(*Convallaria majalis*)
The delicate stems of
bell flowers have
an intense and
delicious fragrance.

PRACTICAL MATTERS

SOIL
Plant in a rich, lime-free potting mixture,
with leafmould added.

SITE
Place in a semi-shady site.

WATERING
Keep the potting mixture moist,
but not soggy.

PLANTS
Grow five dog's tooth violets, twelve snake's
head fritillaries, seven cowslips, one
lithodora, nine lily-of-the-valley, and three
common polypody in a stone sink measuring
120x67x20cm (48x27x8in).

Alpine Selection
✱ In a stone sink that sits in a sunny
position, plant a selection of early-
flowering rockery plants for a spring
display. In late spring, phlox put on a
brilliant show of sweetly scented
blossoms and later the lewisia
produces bright pink flowers.

Snake's head fritillary
(Fritillaria meleagris)
Spring-flowering bulbs
favouring a damp position

Cowslip
(Primula veris)
The nodding trumpets of
sweetly scented flowers
are long-lasting.

Dog's tooth violet
(Erythronium 'Pagoda')
Few flowers have such
poise and beauty of form.

Common polypody
(Polypodium vulgare)
Ferns prefer to grow in
crevices, so this old
piece of bark
suits them.

Mossy floor
A layer of
moss helps
keep the
soil
moist.

MARINE THEME

A GIANT CLAM SHELL may not be the first object that leaps to mind when you are trying to come up with an interesting container, but it makes a magnificent planter for low-growing specimens that do not need a deep root run. This one even had a hole close to its lowest point, solving all drainage problems. The only drawback is its great weight: two people can barely lift it.

❧ Foaming and flowing plants seemed appropriate, and white and silver flowers and foliage add to the marine effect. The flaming Katy introduced a little strong colour, creating just the look I wanted.

❧ The clam could have been planted with alpines, if it was possible to give it protection from excessive damp in winter. Alternatively, a single planting would work effectively: a trailing mound of campanulas *(Campanula garganica)*, a perennial covered by blue flowers in summer; or a carpet of ivy such as 'Duck's Foot Ivy', 'Ivalace', 'Manda's Crested', or the silver-streaked 'Eva'.

Polygonum *(Polygonum affine* 'Donald Lowndes') A mat-forming perennial with deep pink flowers that fade to pale pink.

PRACTICAL MATTERS

SOIL
Plant in a well-drained potting mixture of medium nutritional value and fine gravel (proportions 4:1).

SITE
Place in a sunny site.

WATERING
Take care not to overwater.

PLANTS
Grow two stonecrops, one chamomile, one pink, one heuchera, one polygonum, and two flaming Katy in a 75cm- (30in-) wide and 25cm- (10in-) deep clam shell.

Stonecrop *(Sedum anacampseros)*
A hardy variety with purplish-pink flowers in summer.

Pink (*Dianthus* 'Little Jock')
In summer, this compact
variety bears clove-scented,
single, pale pink flowers with
deep pink centres.

Flaming Katy
(*Kalanchoe blossfeldiana*)
Although this variety is not
hardy, it does well outside
in dry summers.

Chamomile (*Anthemis
punctata cupaniana*)
Grown for the daisy-like flowers
and silver, filigree foliage.

Heuchera (*Heuchera*
'Snowstorm')
A striking variety grown for its
pretty flowers and beautiful,
white leaves edged with green.

Year-round Interest
With the exception of flaming Katy,
all the plants are hardy, and indeed
evergreen, so the arrangement can be left
on constant display all through the year.
It is a planting that changes with the
seasons. Here, we see it in late summer,
when the polygonum is flowering.

WOODEN TROUGH OF EVERGREENS

LOW SHRUBS AND PERENNIALS grow as well as alpines in troughs and sinks, provided they have enough soil. In this 23cm- (9in-) deep, wooden trough, evergreen and silver-leaved plants thrive. The white, winter-flowering heather is less demanding than most ericas, as it tolerates neutral soil. In mild spells in late winter, its flowers may be joined by the lilac-blue ones of the rosemary. A hebe has been introduced for its wonderful, evergreen foliage – later in the year it is covered with white, star-shaped flowers. The curry plant also has flowers in summer, but here it is grown for its magnificent, glistening, silver foliage.

❦ Although this trough has been planted for winter interest, you can replace the winter-flowering heathers with bellflowers or white-flowered, trailing, ivy-leaved pelargoniums during the summer months.

Textured Foliage
❦ A winter arrangement of evergreens, relying on contrasting textures and colours for interest, the planting looks best from above, so place it at ground level, allowing free drainage.

Heather *(Erica carnea* 'Springwood White')
A reliable, winter-flowering variety with white flowers.

Hebe *(Hebe pinguifolia* 'Pagei')
Grown here for its low mound of silvery leaves, this hebe becomes smothered with white flowers in summer.

Ivy *(Hedera helix* 'Ivalace')
Distinguished by its shiny, crinkly, green leaves and prominent veining.

Rosemary *(Rosmarinus officinalis* 'Prostratus') A trailing variety with low foliage and flowers.

Sprawlers in Front
✄ Plant the taller rosemary, hebe, and curry plant at the back of the wooden trough, and then set the heather, ivy, and juniper, which all have a more sprawling habit, towards the front.

PRACTICAL MATTERS

SOIL
Plant in a well-drained, lime-free potting mixture of low nutritional value, mixed with a little gravel (proportions 10:1).

SITE
Place this trough in sunshine.

WATERING
Keep just moist, concentrating the watering on the heathers.

PLANTS
Grow one hebe, two heathers, one ivy, one juniper, and one curry plant in a teak trough, measuring 80x60x20cm (31x23x8in).

Curry plant *(Helichrysum italicum)* Clip regularly but lightly to maintain a round-headed shape.

Creeping juniper *(Juniperus horizontalis* 'Bar Harbor') A low conifer, ideal for troughs.

Wooden and weatherproof Teak troughs are extremely weatherproof, and will last outside for many years without requiring any attention.

Hanging Baskets

THE GREAT ADVANTAGE of hanging baskets is that you can grow small groups of plants in positions that it would be otherwise impossible to consider: high up on a house or on your garden walls, below the branches of a tree, or suspended from the beams of a porch, pergola, arch, or arbour.

— TYPES OF BASKET —

Most commercial hanging baskets are made from a simple, lightweight, wire frame. The fact that the frame is light is important because once they are holding soil and plants they can become quite heavy (always use a lightweight potting mixture). You can improvise, using wicker baskets instead (SEE PAGES 102-3) but they must be strong and firmly attached. Bear in mind that you will not be able to grow plants out of the base of the basket. It will simply be a basket with plants growing out of the top and trailing down the sides.

✻ Several forms of wall basket – which have one flat side so that they can be attached to a vertical surface, easily – are also available, made from terracotta, ceramic, or wire. For a planting on a larger scale, an old hay basket made from iron and secured to a brick or stone wall can look magnificent (SEE PAGES 98-9).

✻ All baskets must be lined before planting. Commercially made liners (constructed from plastic) or fibre pots are available for standard-sized hanging baskets, but I always prefer to see a moss lining – it is less obtrusive and looks so much more natural. Kept moist, it should remain a heathy green all summer. You still need to have a plastic lining, between the moss and the soil, to help retain moisture in the potting mixture. Make sure the layer of moss is even and sufficiently

BALL OF BEGONIAS
Small-leaved, small-flowered bedding begonias, planted to grow into a compact ball of red, white, and pink flowers (ABOVE), last all summer long.

BELOW THE BRANCHES
A basket of busy Lizzies and lobelia (LEFT), suspended from the branches of a tree. Busy Lizzies are an excellent choice for a hanging basket in a shady site.

thick to hide the plastic – sphagnum or carpet moss are the best types for this purpose, and are readily available from garden centres.

— WHICH VIEWPOINT? —

Before choosing the plants for your hanging basket, consider the viewing height for the arrangement. It is no good planning a wonderful top display of flowers if you can only see the bottom of the basket. Choose plants that grow in a way that you will be able to see them well: the ball of flowering begonias (LEFT), for example, can be enjoyed from above, below, and to the side, but the moss baskets (SEE PAGES 102-3) are planted to be seen and admired at about eye-level.

✻ I like to overplant hanging baskets so that they overflow with foliage and flowers. This means watering and feeding them even more frequently than usual through the growing and flowering season: in hot, sunny weather you may have to do it twice or even three times a day. The root balls of the plants can be touching each other, but avoid squashing them into place or they will not have any room to grow.

— HANGING ATTACHMENTS —

When hanging baskets are wet, they can be very heavy and so their fittings need to be extremely strong and secure. Usually, specially designed, metal brackets for attaching to vertical surfaces are sold with hanging baskets. Secure the bracket firmly to the wall with screws and rawl plugs. If you are suspending a basket from a pergola or porch, make sure that you hang it from a sturdy and stout crossbar. Every time you hang up a basket planted with a new arrangement, check that the fittings, the bracket, and the chain are all safe and secure.

TRADITIONAL BASKET

ALTHOUGH HANGING BASKETS can be planted for every season of the year, it is in summer that they really come into their own. Low and trailing annuals with a profusion of flowers, such as pelargoniums, petunias, begonias, sweet alyssum, blue lobelia, and busy Lizzies have become favourite plants to use in baskets – and for good reason. They all give a continuous show of colour from early summer until the first frosts. Many other plants also do well, including convolvulus, verbena, nasturtium, lantana, lotus, portulaca, calceolaria, and felicia, but only the verbena and nasturtium have the same staying power as the first stalwart group.

PRACTICAL MATTERS

SOIL
Plant in a lightweight potting mixture of medium nutritional value.

SITE
Hang in a sunny site.

WATERING
Keep well watered, especially in hot weather. Feed weekly.

PLANTS
Grow six lobelias, four helichrysum, two sweet alyssum, two portulaca, three ivy-leaved pelargoniums, and three calceolaria in a 35cm- (14in-) diameter, moss-lined, wire hanging basket.

PLANTING UP A HANGING BASKET

1 Line the basket with sphagnum moss, so that it covers the inside of the basket completely but is not so thick that it takes up valuable root space for the plants.

2 Place a plastic liner over the moss so that the planting will not dry out too quickly. Trim to neaten. If you are not growing plants through the base, cut five drainage holes in the plastic.

3 If you wish to encourage trailing plants to grow out of the bottom of the basket, carefully wrap each in a small piece of plastic, shaped into a narrow cone. Cover the roots with the wide end of the cone and the leaves with the narrow part.

Portulaca *(Portulaca grandiflora)*
A sun lover, available in pinks, reds, and white.

4 Pierce a hole in the base of the lining. From the inside, thread the narrow end of the cone through the hole. Pull through until the leafy part of the plant is outside the basket, pull the plastic cone away, leaving the plant in position. Repeat.

5 When you have a ring of plants around the base, fill the basket with 7.5cm (3in) of potting mixture. Thread through more trailing plants and firm soil around their roots. Complete another ring before you reach the top.

Helichrysum
(Helichrysum petiolare)
A useful, trailing, foliage plant for hanging baskets.

6 Plant the top of the basket with a mixture of trailing and bushy plants, and then fill with potting mixture, making sure that the final level of the soil is just below the top, to allow for watering. Hang the basket in its permanent position and water well.

• Calceolaria
(Calceolaria
'Sunshine')
A compact,
bushy plant
with vibrant
yellow
flowers.

**• Ivy-leaved
pelargonium**
(Pelargonium
'Madame Crousse')
A pale pink
flowered variety.

**Sweet
alyssum**
*(Lobularia
maritima*
'Little Dorrit')
Adds a hint of
white to the
planting.

Non-stop Flowers
Four weeks later,
the plants have grown
considerably and the
first flowers are opening.
The pelargoniums, sweet
alyssum, calceolaria,
lobelias, and portulaca
will continue to flower
until autumn as long as
you remove the dead
blooms. The portulaca
flowers open only in the
sun. Clip the helichrysum
if it grows too large.

• Lobelia *(Lobelia erinus*
'Cascade Mixture')
A very floriferous variety,
with flowers in shades of
lilac, pink, carmine, and white.

GOLD SUMMER BASKET

A BASKET OF GOLDEN FLOWERS and foliage makes a beautiful hanging feature in a semi-shady spot that needs cheering up. I find that loose, less considered plantings usually work best in hanging baskets, but occasionally, a calculated, close colour scheme looks just right. The informality of the helichrysum, mixed with yellow and gold pansies, golden ivy, and yellow snapdragons creates a natural, wild-looking arrangement.

PRACTICAL MATTERS

SOIL
Plant in a rich, lightweight potting mixture.

SITE
Place in a sheltered, semi-shady or sunny site.

WATERING
Keep well watered and feed twice a week.

PLANTS
Grow three helichrysum, three golden ivy, six pansies (three of each variety), and four snapdragons in a 35cm- (14in-) diameter, wire hanging basket lined with moss and plastic.

Pansy (*Viola* Crystal Bowl Series) The clear yellow flowers have a delicious scent.

Pansy (*Viola* x *wittrockiana* 'Rhine Gold') Do not allow the plants to become straggly or their flowering will be impaired.

Snapdragon (*Antirrhinum* 'Sweetheart') Any low-growing, yellow-flowered variety would be suitable for this basket.

Threading Trick
✄ To encourage plants to grow in all directions, I threaded some ivy and two pansies through the base of the basket. The other plants were put in the top. As a general rule, you should only thread trailing or short plants through the base.

Golden ivy (*Hedera helix* 'Harald') The leaves are gold-edged.

Helichrysum (*Helichrysum petiolare* 'Aureum') A very fast grower, this annual needs to be kept under control with an occasional trim.

BASKET OF RED AND SILVER

CLASHING REDS WORK TOGETHER in a fascinating way. Pink-red and orange-red intensify each other when placed close together, and set against the delicate, feathery, silver foliage of the lotus, they look wonderful. I felt a little relief was needed, and so introduced two coleus plants for the gold in their leaves.

PRACTICAL MATTERS

SOIL
Plant in a rich, lightweight potting mixture.

SITE
Place in a sunny site.

WATERING
Water well, never allowing the basket to dry out. Feed twice a week.

PLANTS
Grow two 'Yale' ivy-leaved pelargoniums, one 'Tavira' ivy-leaved pelargonium, three portulaca, four verbena, four lotus, and two coleus in a 45cm- (18in-) diameter, wire hanging basket, lined with moss and plastic.

Verbena (*Verbena* x *hybrida* 'Showtime')
A bushy perennial grown as an annual with serrated foliage and brilliant red flowers.

Coleus (*Coleus blumei*)
Choose red and crimson varieties with a splash of gold.

Portulaca (*Portulaca grandiflora* Sundance Series)
A semi-trailing annual with double, rose-like flowers.

Ivy-leaved pelargonium (*Pelargonium* 'Tavira')
Stems of delicate, crimson, flowers trail from the basket.

Ivy-leaved pelargonium (*Pelargonium* 'Yale')
The velvety flowers are a magnificent, dark red.

Lotus (*Lotus berthelotii*)
A tender perennial useful for its silvery foliage and red, pea like flowers, which are not yet out in this arrangement.

Dash of Red
✻ This hanging basket will have a long flowering life, for the pelargoniums and verbenas will continue to flower until the frosts.

HAYRACK OF FLOWERS

WALL BASKETS ARE PARTICULARLY USEFUL in tight places where a circular basket will not fit. They are only half the width of hanging baskets, with flat backs that can be attached to a wall, usually by slotting them on to two screws protruding from the wall. Originally used for holding hay in horse stables, hayracks are the same shape as a half basket, but they are larger and made with iron bars. They make excellent planters for the garden, so much so that reproductions are now sold specifically for garden plants.

The arrangement in this hayrack is designed for a position just above eye-level on a shady wall. The fuchsias and begonias will grow more and more, tumbling down the sides as summer advances and autumn arrives. To achieve this effect, when planting, slightly lean the plants in the direction that you want them to grow, and position some trailers between the bars. As with conventional hanging baskets, I have lined this hayrack with moss and plastic, so I had to make holes in the lining to thread through some plants and provide drainage.

PRACTICAL MATTERS

SOIL
Plant in a rich, lightweight potting mixture.

SITE
Place in a shady or semi-shady site.

WATERING
Keep well watered and feed once a week.

PLANTS
Grow three begonias, three fuchsias, and two busy Lizzies in a 50cm (20in) hayrack.

• **Busy Lizzies** (*Impatiens* New Guinea hybrid) White-flushed, pink flowers open amidst bronze leaves, veined with vibrant orange and yellow streaks.

Colour Choice

This rich, deep pink, dark purple, and pale pink mix would look particularly effective against a dark, brick wall, where the glowing colours would brighten the shade for several months in summer. The following season use the same plants, but try different colour combinations: amber begonias, orange busy Lizzies with dark red leaves, and red fuchsias; or ice-pink begonias with gold-leaved, white busy Lizzies, and a fuchsia such as 'Pink Galore'.

• **Fuchsia** (*Fuchsia* 'Gruss aus dem Bodenthal') Bears a profusion of bright pink flowers with deep purple tubes.

• **Begonia** (*Begonia* x *tuberhybrida* 'Roy Hartley') A semi-pendulous form with scrumptious, long-lasting, cerise-coloured flowers.

CLASHING-COLOURED ANNUALS

HUNDREDS OF PANSY VARIETIES are available to the gardener in the most beautiful colours, providing you with enormous scope for exciting colour combinations. You can buy pansies at almost any time of the year, but the summer-flowering varieties are the most floriferous. Whenever you grow them, they need attention. Deadhead, and after heavy flowering, cut the plants back to stop them becoming leggy and to promote new growth.

PRACTICAL MATTERS

SOIL
Plant in a well-drained, lightweight potting mixture of high nutritional value.

SITE
Place in a semi-shady site.

WATERING
Water and feed frequently.

PLANTS
Grow eight pansies, five alyssum, three monkey flowers, three wandering Jews, and two plectranthrus in a 45cm- (18in-) diameter, moss-lined, wire hanging basket.

Plectranthus
(*Plectranthus coleoides* 'Variegatus')
Remove the spires of flowers for the best display of variegated foliage.

Monkey flower
(*Mimulus* hybrids)
Deadhead frequently.

Wandering Jew
(*Tradescantia fluminensis* 'Variegata')
An indoor plant, ideal as a trailer in summer.

Pansy (*Viola* 'Jolly Joker')
Produces masses of flowers all summer.

Sphere of Colour
⚘ This hanging basket will be a ball of colour for months. The colour scheme is as beautiful as it is unusual. To achieve the effect, thread plants into the base of the basket, and then arange the others on top.

Sweet alyssum
(*Lobularia maritima* 'Wonderland')
A fast-growing annual.

SPRING COLLECTION

SPRING IS THE HIGH POINT of this planting, although it will also look attractive in winter and summer. The evergreen foliage of the euonymus and spurge provides winter interest before the little daisies start to open from mid winter onwards. The daisy flowers are joined by windflowers and pasque flowers in late spring, and also the spurge. Deadhead the daisies and they will continue to flower in summer, against the silver spurge.

PRACTICAL MATTERS

SOIL
Plant in a lightweight potting mixture of medium nutritional value.

SITE
Place in a sunny position, sheltered from strong winds.

WATERING
Keep just moist.

PLANTS
Grow eight double daisies, three pasque flowers, twelve windflowers, three spurges, and three euonymus in a 40cm- (16in-) diameter, moss-lined, wire basket.

Windflower
(*Anemone blanda* 'White Splendour')
A tuberous, spring-flowering plant.

Euonymus
(*Euonymus fortunei* 'Emerald 'n' Gold')
A useful, evergreen shrub for any container planting.

Eye-level Viewing
✘ To appreciate this pretty pink, white, and lime-green planting of bulbs and early-flowering perennials, hang the basket at eye-level or even lower in a sunny site. Plant it in the autumn, so that you can enjoy it as the display changes through the winter, spring, and summer.

Double daisy
(*Bellis perennis*)
Deadhead to encourage a long-lasting flower display.

Pasque flower (*Pulsatilla vulgaris* 'Rubra')
The yellow anthers accentuate the rich colour of the petals.

Spurge (*Euphorbia myrsinites*)
A spreading sun lover with lime-green flowers.

MOSS BASKETS

THIS BLAZING, YELLOW TRIO of favourite spring flowers grows in three moss baskets, attached to each other to make an unusual hanging container. I secured the three basket handles together in two places with garden wire: at the point where the handles join the basket, and 13cm (5in) further up the handles, just before they start to curve towards the centre. I wired the chain in at the same time, securing it at both the points. Each of the baskets is lined with plastic, pricked in the bottom for drainage, and then filled with a lightweight potting mixture, which will not put too much strain on the baskets or the chain.

Polyanthus (*Primula*
Pacific hybrids)
These will flower sporadically
in mild spells from late winter
until late spring.

—— PLANTING PLAN ——

I planted both the daffodil and tulip bulbs in late autumn. The polyanthus, which are available from florists as well as garden centres, can be planted from autumn onwards; in especially cold areas it is best to wait until early spring or they may be damaged by frost. All the plants are hardy and will need to be only lightly watered during the winter months to keep the potting mixture just moist. Do not water in frosty weather.

—— LONG-LASTING FLOWERS ——

If kept in semi-shade, the arrangement should remain in flower for several weeks in mid spring; in a sunny spot the daffodils and tulips might come out and finish more quickly but the polyanthus will continue flowering sporadically until late spring.

PRACTICAL MATTERS

SOIL
Plant in a well-drained, lightweight potting mixture
of medium nutritional value.

SITE
Hang this arrangement in semi-shade for the best
effect, although the plants will grow in a
sunny or shady site.

WATERING
Keep lightly watered through the winter, so the soil
does not become too dry.

PLANTS
Grow five polyanthus and twelve tulips each in two
30cm- (12in-) diameter, moss baskets, and twelve
narcissi in a 18cm- (7in-) diameter, moss basket.

Tulip (*Tulipa* 'Monte Carlo') A double-flowered variety reaching 30cm (12in) tall.

Daffodil (*Narcissus* 'April Tears') A delicate, pale-yellow daffodil with a strong fragrance.

Unusual touch Moss baskets secured together with garden wire and suspended on a chain make an unusual hanging basket.

Joys of Spring

The bright, rich yellows of the flowers in this unusual hanging basket epitomize spring. Hang it against a house, a fence, or a wall in semi-shade for long-lasting flowers.

SUITING THE SITE

❧

ALWAYS ASSESS THE AMOUNT of sun, wind, and cold a site receives before deciding what to grow there, but also think about the aesthetics: the shape, colour, and texture of the proposed planting and the character and size of the container, in relation to its immediate surroundings.

UNDER THE EAVES OF A POTTING SHED
Astilbes and begonias, both summer-flowering plants, like a spot in dappled shade, away from the harsh glare of the sun.

SUNNY POSITIONS

THE MAJORITY OF PLANTS love sunshine. Good light and lots of sun makes them grow into strong specimens with healthy green leaves and an abundance of flowers. However, it can be too much of a good thing, and if plants in containers receive very hot sun all day, they dry out extremely quickly. In hot, sunny spells, when plants in containers are subjected to constant sun, you may need to water them two or three times a day. Even then, it is possible that the leaves may become scorched and yellow and the flowers deformed from excess sun, so if you have a very sunny garden, choose plants renowned for their robust qualities and endurance in hot weather.

—— INTENSE HEAT ——

Cacti and succulents, aloe, cordylines, yuccas, and agave all thrive in baking conditions – extreme sun and little water. Conveniently, they will also put up with low temperatures, at least down to freezing in winter. They dislike a mixture of cold and damp, so if such conditions are likely, it is safest to bring them into a conservatory or greenhouse over winter. When the weather improves in late spring, bring them outside for the open-air sunbathing they so enjoy.

—— VIBRANT COLOUR ——

A riot of brilliant colour suits a sunny site. Flowering plants, such as zonal and regal pelargoniums, thrive in such conditions, as do snapdragons, petunias, marigolds, salvias, gazanias, helichrysum, hibiscus, pinks, phlox, and zinnias. All bloom over a long period, starting in early summer and continuing until the first

PROVENCE-STYLE
Trailing pelargoniums, planted in an oil jar from the south of France (ABOVE), spell out sunshine. In ideal, Mediterranean conditions, pelargoniums reach 6m (20ft) tall, but only if grown in the open ground. A container restricts their height.

CACTUS GARDEN
A terracotta-tiled terrace (LEFT), where cereus and prickly pear grow in large clay pots, casting their dramatic shadows against a white wall. Echeverias and stonecrops grow around the base of the prickly pear.

frosts. In warm climates, pelargoniums, petunias, pinks, and gazanias can be grown as perennials and left outside.

Most of these flowering plants come in a wide range of coloured varieties. I like to plant a glorious mixture of them together in large containers, such as tubs and barrels, to make the most of their exuberant colour. Do not overfeed them during the flowering season or they will produce too much foliage and only a few flowers.

—— HEADY FRAGRANCE ——

I always try to have plenty of containers with fragrant flowers or foliage positioned beside a doorway or garden seat. Scented, flowering plants for sunny situations include pinks, lavender, some verbenas, sweet alyssum, mignonette, several varieties of petunia, and, of course, roses. Although roses thrive in sun, they need a moist root run, so plant them where it does not become too hot: halfway between sun and semi-shade is best.

Aromatic foliage plants, such as rosemary, artemisia, lemon verbena, lemon balm, chamomile, and several pelargoniums – all natives of the Mediterranean – also thrive in hot conditions. Plant each species in its own pot, and arrange them randomly in a group on a sunny patio where they can be enjoyed for their scented leaves.

—— FRUIT TREES ——

Many trees grow well in large containers in a sunny position. They need feeding during their growing season and copious watering in hot spells. Dwarf fruit trees, such as apples, pears, and plums, are all suitable and will produce a respectable crop.

FLOWER-FILLED PERGOLA

As the focal point at the end of a long, narrow, town garden, this pergola calls out for eye-catching planting schemes. It was only built three months ago so the climbers have not yet covered the pillars and cross beams. This presented a marvellous opportunity to furnish it with pots of colourful annuals and roses for the summer.

✼ Reconstituted stone baskets and terracotta pots with pink-flowered pelargoniums, busy Lizzies, eustoma, and a bright patch of gold coleus rest on the stone-paved floor, providing colour just above ground level. In sun, all of these plants flower non-stop and demand minimum care. With breeders always bringing out new varieties of pelargoniums, it is impossible to tire of them.

✼ The roses in the weathered, ornamental terracotta pots on either side of the steps leading to the pergola are very floriferous. 'Ballerina' starts later than other roses but makes up for this by going on non-stop until the frosts. Deadhead all the time to encourage it to throw out more sprays of flower buds.

HIGH-LEVEL INTEREST

Pergolas present excellent opportunities for using hanging baskets, brimming over with trailing, summer-flowering annuals. Suspended on the left-hand side of the pergola, red pelargoniums, verbena, and lotus burst from a traditional basket, creating a glorious red ball all summer long. (For details on planting the basket SEE PAGE 97.) More colour is added at shoulder height with three standard pelargoniums. Although they must not be overwatered, they need a surprising amount of moisture in hot weather.

IN THE WINTER

This is very much a summer display. In autumn and winter, when the annuals are over, you could decorate the pergola with evergreen bay, box, and privet, trained and clipped into standards, neat spheres, and cones. A hanging basket of golden ivy would contrast well with their dark green foliage.

Zonal pelargonium *(Pelargonium* 'Yale') The flowers are a stunning, deep, velvety, blood red.

Lotus *(Lotus berthelotii)* An ideal annual for a hanging basket, with its fine, trailing, silver foliage and red flowers.

Verbena *(Verbena* x *hybrida* 'Showtime') A variety that comes in a range of colours, although I used only red ones here.

Portulaca *(Portulaca grandiflora* 'Sundance Series') Sun is essential for the pretty flowers to open.

Verbena *(Verbena* x *hybrida* 'Silver Anne') A pretty pink variety, chosen to echo the colours of the pelargonium.

Zonal pelargonium *(Pelargonium* 'Rio') A recent, pale pink variety with deep pink eyes.

Polyantha rose *(Rosa* 'Margot Koster') A variety that is strongly recommended for growing in containers.

Plants in a sunny site must be watered frequently. In hot, summer weather this may mean up to two or three times a day. Bear in mind that hanging baskets are especially likely to dry out because they hold so little potting mixture. Although the hanging basket has a plastic liner behind the moss to conserve moisture, it still needs constant attention. Give the plants a liquid feed once a week throughout the summer. In hot weather, plants in containers are more susceptible to mildew, as the soil dries out. When you see the first signs of mildew, spray with a fungicide.

Zonal pelargonium
(*Pelargonium* 'Mauritania')
Distinguished by ice-pink flowers with deep pink centres, it is fast-growing, which makes it an excellent standard.

Zonal pelargonium
(*Pelargonium* 'Appleblossom Rosebud')
The beautiful, two-tone flowers dislike wet weather.

Rose (*Rosa* 'The Fairy')
A pretty variety bearing dense clusters of small, double flowers.

Zonal pelargonium
(*Pelargonium* 'Ivalo')
The rich pink flowers have centres of an even deeper pink.

Rose (*Rosa* 'Ballerina')
After a late start, this variety is seldom out of flower in summer.

Coleus (*Coleus blumei*)
Clip back regularly to maintain a bushy mound of colourful foliage.

Eustoma (*Eustoma grandiflora*)
Violet- and white-flowered varieties are available, as well as the pink ones used here.

Busy Lizzy (*Impatiens* 'New Guinea hybrid')
A striking variety with pink flowers and dark red leaves.

SCHEMES FOR SUN

MANY OF THE PLANTS THAT THRIVE in sunny sites give colour for several months of the year. The most widely planted group are the summer annuals. In late spring and early summer, garden centres and nurseries are stacked with the usual and beautiful run of petunias, pelargoniums, snapdragons, salvias, lobelias, marigolds, and sweet alyssum. It is a good idea to devise a colour scheme for your containers well in advance of going to buy the plants. Combinations that I find work well together are bluey pinks with silver-leaved plants; clear blues with pale yellows and lime green; and the orange, red, and apricot range. Violet, lilac, and mauve also look good against silver foliage, and yellow and ice-pink make an interesting pair. Alternatively, mix a great many colours in just one scheme.

❧ Winter calls for bright-leaved, evergreen shrubs. Gold foliage plants always look cheerful, even in grey weather, so use euonymus, aucuba, variegated fatsia, privet, elaeagnus, box, and yew. Among spring bulbs, all narcissi, tulips, hyacinths, and crocuses grow happily in sun. I favour the most heavily scented ones for containers.

Pink Splash
❧ Regal pelargoniums excel in a sunny site (ABOVE), although their bright flowers are easily damaged in wet and windy weather. Their vibrant colour is strengthened by the green background.

Pure Simplicity
❧ It is hard to beat the simple beauty of a sun-loving, white chamomile (*Anthemis punctata cupaniana*) in a plain, terracotta pot (LEFT).

Water Garden
❧ A small water garden (RIGHT) holds miniature water lilies (*Nymphaea pygmaea* 'Helvola'), water lettuce (*Pistia stratiotes*), and water hyacinth (*Eichhornia acicularis*). The roots of the water lilies must be 15cm (6in) below the surface. The floaters are tender, but the lilies will survive the winter, as long as the water does not freeze solid.

PLANTS FOR SUN

ZINNIA
(Zinnia elegans)

THE VAST MAJORITY OF PLANTS are sun lovers, especially those that produce a multitude of flowers. Annuals in particular like to bask in the sun, growing luxuriantly in its rays. In very hot summers, though, the heat can be too strong for even the most avid sun lovers, even scorching those that are kept well watered. If possible, move the containers to a position where they get some respite from the hottest, midday sun.

DELPHINIUM
(Delphinium elatum 'Sungleam')

PETUNIA
(Petunia Ruffles Series)

EUSTOMA
(Eustoma grandiflorum)

ᔒ SPRING ᔒ

Auricula *(Primula auricula)*
Broom *(Cytisus)*
Cineraria *(Senecio* x *hybridus)*
Crocus *(Crocus)*
Crown imperial *(Fritillaria imperialis)*
Double daisy *(Bellis perennis)*
Flowering cherry *(Prunus)*
Forget-me-not *(Myosotis)*
Glory-of-the-snow *(Chionodoxa)*
Grape hyacinth *(Muscari)*
Hyacinth *(Hyacinthus)*
Iris *(Iris)*
Narcissus *(Narcissus)*
Pasque flower *(Pulsatilla vulgaris)*
Persian buttercup *(Ranunculus asiaticus)*
Phlox *(Phlox subulata)*
Polyanthus *(Primula vulgaris* hybrids)
Saxifrage *(Saxifraga)*
Spring gentian *(Gentiana verna)*
Spurge *(Euphorbia)*
Squill *(Scilla)*
Tulip *(Tulipa)*
Wallflower *(Cheiranthus)*
Weigela *(Weigela)*
Windflower *(Anemone)*

———————— • ————————

ᔒ SUMMER ᔒ

Abutilon *(Abutilon)*
African lily *(Agapanthus)*
Asparagus *(Asparagus)*
Black-eyed Susan *(Thunbergia alata)*
Calceolaria *(Calceolaria)*
Celosia *(Celosia cristata)*
Chamomile *(Anthemis)*
Chrysanthemum *(Chrysanthemum)*
Cigar flower *(Cuphea ignea)*
Coleus *(Coleus blumei)*
Common rue *(Ruta graveolens)*
Convolvulus *(Convolvulus cneorum)*
Corn cockle *(Agrostemma)*
Courgette
Delphinium *(Delphinium elatum)*
Diascia *(Diascia)*
Eustoma *(Eustoma)*
Flaming Katy *(Kalanchoe)*
Floss flower *(Ageratum)*
French marigold *(Tagetes)*
Gazania *(Gazania)*
Godetia *(Clarkia)*
Gypsophila *(Gypsophila)*
Halimiocistus (x *Halimiocistus)*
Helichrysum *(Helichrysum)*
Heliotrope *(Heliotropium)*
Houseleek *(Sempervivum)*
Lantana *(Lantana)*
Lavender *(Lavandula)*
Livingstone daisy *(Mesembryanthemum)*

HOUTTUYNIA
(Houttuynia cordata 'Chamaeleon')

MICHAELMAS DAÏSY
(Aster)

VERBENA
(Verbena 'Sissinghurst')

GLADIOLUS
(Gladiolus hybrid)

LADY'S MANTLE
(Alchemilla mollis)

LAVENDER
(Lavandula lanata)

Lobelia *(Lobelia)*
Lotus *(Lotus berthelotii)*
Mallow *(Lavatera)*
Marjoram *(Origanum)*
Monkey flower *(Mimulus)*
Nasturtium *(Tropaeolum majus)*
Nemesia *(Nemesia)*
Onion *(Allium)*
Pansy *(Viola)*
Parsley *(Petroselinum crispum)*
Pelargonium *(Pelargonium)*
Pentas *(Pentas)*
Petunia *(Petunia* x *hybrida)*
Plecostachys *(Plecostachys)*
Plumbago *(Plumbago)*
Poppy *(Papaver)*
Portulaca *(Portulaca)*
Potentilla *(Potentilla)*
Rock rose *(Cistus)*
Rose *(Rosa)*
Sage *(Salvia)*
Santolina *(Santolina)*
Scabious *(Scabiosa)*
Senecio *(Senecio maritima)*
Snapdragon *(Antirrhinum)*
Southernwood *(Artemisia)*
Spurge *(Euphorbia)*
Stock *(Mathiola)*
Stonecrop *(Sedum)*
Strawberry *(Fragaria)*
Sweet alyssum *(Lobularia maritima)*
Sweet pea *(Lathyrus)*
Thyme *(Thymus)*
Venidio (x *Venidio-arctotis)*
Verbena *(Verbena)*
Wandering Jew *(Tradescantia)*
Water lily *(Nymphaea)*
Yucca *(Yucca)*
Zinnia *(Zinnia elegans)*

⤳ **AUTUMN** ⤳

Ceratostigma *(Ceratostigma)*
Chrysanthemum *(Chrysanthemum)*
Dahlia *(Dahlia)*
Gladiolus *(Gladiolus)*
Heather *(Calluna)*
Hebe *(Hebe)*
Houttuynia *(Houttuynia)*
Kaffir lily *(Schizostylis)*
Nasturtium *(Tropaeolum majus)*
Nerine *(Nerine bowdenii)*
Pernettya *(Pernettya mucronata)*
Tomato

⸻ • ⸻

⤳ **WINTER** ⤳

Box *(Buxus)*
Conifers
Crocus *(Crocus)*
Daphne *(Daphne mezereum)*
Euonymus *(Euonymus fortunei)*
Helichrysum *(Helichrysum italicum)*
Heather *(Erica)*
Ivy *(Hedera helix)*
Ornamental cabbage
(Brassica oleracea)
Pansy *(Viola)*
Polyanthus *(Primula hybrids)*
Rosemary *(Rosmarinus)*
Winter aconite *(Eranthis hyemalis)*
Winter cherry *(Solanum capsicastrum)*
Winter iris *(Iris unguicularis)*

⸻ • ⸻

Most of the plants recommended for
winter are evergreens, and so provide
year-round
interest.

PETUNIA
(Petunia Ruffles
Series)

AFRICAN LILY
*(Agapanthus
campanulatus)*

ROSE
(Rosa 'The Fairy')

MARANTA
*(Maranta
leuconeura)*

SEMI-SHADY POSITIONS

T HE SEMI-SHADY garden gets the best of both worlds: it escapes the rigours of full sun beating down throughout the day, and yet does not have the rather depressing and gloomy feel of unrelieved shade. Plants love semi-shade. They receive enough sun to make them grow and flower well, and sufficient shade to prevent them from drying out too fast, or being burnt and scorched by over-exposure to heat.

— IDEAL SEATING AREA —

Most gardens include areas of semi-shade: if you live in a detached house you will have two or more walls that only see the sun for part of the day. If you are designing your garden, and you can choose where your paved sitting area near the house will be, allocate it a semi-shady position. You can always take a chair out into a sunny place on the lawn if you want sunlight. Preferably choose a site that receives the morning sun, because breakfast is the one meal of the day that can be enjoyed in a sunny place – by lunch time the sun is often too strong. If you already have a sunny sitting area, you could plant a tree, placing it judiciously, so that the area is in dappled shade for at least part of the day. Some of my happiest moments have been spent sitting in the dappled, early-morning sunshine under an old apple tree, beside a path edged with pots of lavender, rosemary, and southernwood, having a breakfast of homemade breads and conserves with coffee.

— CITY BENEFITS —

In the city, nearby buildings usually cast shadows on small paved gardens or roof terraces for part of the day. Unless you live in an extremely cold

WILD GARDEN
A bulbous, terracotta pot (ABOVE) filled with a wild jumble of pansies, bellflowers, cranesbill, and ferns.

FLOWER BASKETS
Placed on a sun-warmed, stone bench, baskets of pansies, columbine, a pick a back plant, bellflowers, and a small clipped mop-head of box, thrive in the dappled sun (LEFT).

area, there will be plenty of scope for having a year-round backdrop of greenery, achieved by growing evergreen shrubs in good-sized containers.

Temperatures in cities are always a few degrees higher than those in the surrounding countryside, which gives you a wider choice of plants to grow in containers. Walls will become warmed by only a few hours of sunshine and they will retain the heat over several hours, so that even in winter the area at the base of the wall is substantially warmer than a site that is just a few yards away. Take advantage of this shelter and warmth to try growing some of the slightly more tender, exotic-looking, garden plants.

— PASTEL COLOURS —

Furnish a semi-shady, paved terrace with containers filled with all manner of greenery and coloured flowers. Always have some perfumed plants, whether it be species with aromatic leaves or ones with fragrant flowers. They appeal to more than one of our senses and make the atmosphere much more interesting and special.

Whereas green is usually the predominant colour for shady sites, and a mixture of hot, bright colours can be exciting for sunny places, I like semi-shady container plantings based on flowers with pastel colours. To me, they look wonderful in a site that is neither too bright nor too dark. Spring bulbs, flowering shrubs, perennials, and summer annuals and biennials all offer a range of gentle, clear shades: pinks and lemons, lilacs and mauves, peach, pale orange, and sky blue. All these colours blend well with each other, either as a glorious mixture, or in a more restricted, carefully selected palette for a soothing arrangement.

CITY COURTYARD

THIS TERRACE in the heart of the city sees sun for only part of the day because of the high boundary walls and surrounding buildings. What might seem a disadvantage initially, however, can be an asset: as the area is sheltered, tender plants such as aspidistras survive outside all-year-round in the temperate climate.

The terrace is on view from inside the house, so I have planted a mixture of evergreen plants, such as yucca and New Zealand flax, to which I can add seasonal colour. Seen here in early summer, the dramatic hosta by the steps has just grown its new leaves. The scented wallflowers beside it are nearly over but summer annuals are just getting underway. Against a backdrop of cool greens, the busy Lizzies, fuchsias, begonias, and violas will produce plentiful colour in summer and autumn.

Wallflower (*Cheiranthus cheiri*) •
These popular yellow, red, and pink-flowered biennials have the most glorious scent.

Hosta (*Hosta sieboldiana* 'Frances Williams') •
The magnificent gold-edged leaves of this hosta fill the dark corner next to the stone steps.

Aspidistra (*Aspidistra elatior*) •
In the wild, its flowers at the base of the leaves are pollinated by snails.

Rhododendron (*Rhododendron* 'Grumpy') •
This impressive, acid-loving plant flowers in late spring but it may also have a few autumn blooms.

Busy Lizzie (*Impatiens walleriana* 'Tangeglow')
The orange flowers have long spurs.

Pansy (*Viola* x *wittrockiana*)
The rich red flowers stand out well against the pale green garden seat.

PLANT CARE

Container-grown plants in semi-shade require more attention than those grown in sun. Water to keep the potting mixture moist but not wet, remove dead leaves and flowers, and feed during the growing season.

- **Begonia** (*Begonia* x *tuberhybrida*)
Grown as annuals, these flower continuously through summer and autumn. Water well and feed once a week.

- **Fuchsia** (*Fuchsia* 'Autumnale')
A variety combining beautiful pink-tinged, cream, and green variegated foliage, with bright pink flowers in summer and autumn.

- **Holly fern** (*Phanerophlebia falcata*)
A slightly tender fern, best grown in a potting mixture rich in leafmould.

- **New Zealand flax** (*Phormium tenax* 'Variegatum')
This decorative evergreen plant appreciates the sunniest spot.

- **Busy Lizzie**
(*Impatiens walleriana*)
These flower non-stop through summer and autumn, if watered plentifully and given a weekly feed.

- **Ivy** (*Hedera helix* 'Eva')
Cascading down from the container, shade-loving ivy will live for many years.

- **Male fern**
(*Dryopteris filix-mas*)
This semi-evergreen fern produces arching fronds over 1m (3ft) long.

- **Yucca** (*Yucca gloriosa*)
A hardy plant that lasts many years when grown in a container.

SCHEMES FOR SEMI-SHADE

NEARLY ALL THE PLANTS that are regarded as sun lovers, as well as those that prefer shade, can be grown in semi-shade, so there is no shortage of species from which to choose. It is the business of combining them that can be restrictive. Plants in one container must all like the same soil type and have similar watering requirements. Watering should not present too much of a problem as most plants like to be kept moist but not soggy. Soil demands can be more limiting, however, as certain plants only grow well, either in alkaline or acid soil conditions.

——— ACID OR ALKALINE? ———

An interesting grouping of alkaline-loving plants for a large container could consist of the shrub Mexican orange blossom – either the gold-leaved variety 'Sundance' or the fine-leaved 'Aztec Pearl'

– with fuchsias and evergreen ivies. Mexican orange blossom, an evergreen shrub, can grow quite large so the container needs to be about 50cm (20in) in diameter. If your garden is not too cold, you could use hardy fuchsias, such as the variety 'Mrs Popple', to make a permanent container planting.

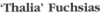 Rhododendrons, azaleas, and camellias are excellent container specimens for a half-shady position, and all prefer an acid potting mixture. Rhododendrons and camellias grow quite large, so there will be little room for other plants, apart from, perhaps, some spring bulbs and small ivies around the edge of the containers. All three acid-loving shrubs flower in late spring and early summer, but the glossy leaves of most of them form an evergreen backdrop throughout the year. Camellias have the most attractive foliage, but they are the least hardy of the trio.

'Thalia' Fuchsias
An old, lead tank makes a very special container for these small-flowered fuchsias (*Fuchsia* 'Thalia') with their dark foliage and deep orange bells (LEFT). The plants grow quickly in a partly shady place, given plenty of water and a weekly feed. They start to flower a little later than most fuchsias but continue until the first frosts.

Evergreen Curtain
Pots and bowls of pastel-coloured busy Lizzies (*Impatiens walleriana*) and begonias (*Begonia* X *tuberhybrida*), mixed with maidenhair ferns (*Adiantum capillus-veneris*) and variegated ivy (*Hedera helix* 'Dealbata'), set against a curtain of evergreen shrubs (RIGHT). All the plants grow amazingly well on this terrace in a town garden, which receives dappled sun for much of the day.

PLANTS FOR SEMI-SHADE

YOU WILL HAVE LITTLE PROBLEM finding plants that do well in a semi-shady position but you first need to establish what degree of shade you have in your garden. If the light is always bright and there is the possibility of sun for half the day, most shrubs, perennials, and annuals will thrive. If the shade is deep with a shorter period of dappled sun, then woodland plants, such as hellebores, hydrangeas, lilies, rhododendrons and azaleas, and camellias generally do best.

FUCHSIA
(*Fuchsia* 'Pink Galore')

BLEEDING HEART
(*Dicentra spectabilis*)

✐ WINTER ✐

Aucuba (*Aucuba*)
Bamboos
Bergenia (*Bergenia*)
Box (*Buxus*)
Conifers
Euonymus (*Euonymus*)
Fatsia (*Fatsia*)
Gaultheria (*Gaultheria*)
Hellebore (*Helleborus niger*)
Ivy (*Hedera helix*)
Laurestinus (*Viburnum tinus*)
Leucothöe (*Leucothöe*)
Mexican orange blossom (*Choisya*)
Pansy (*Viola*)
Periwinkle (*Vinca*)
Skimmia (*Skimmia*)
Winter cherry (*Solanum capsicastrum*)

———— • ————

Most of the plants recommended for winter are evergreens, and therefore provide year-round interest.

✐ SPRING ✐

Auricula (*Primula auricula*)
Azalea/Rhododendron (*Rhododendron*)
Camellia (*Camellia*)
Cowslip (*Primula veris*)
Crown imperial (*Fritillaria imperialis*)
Daffodil (*Narcissus*)
Forget-me-not (*Myosotis*)
Grape hyacinth (*Muscari*)
Hellebore (*Helleborus*)
Hyacinth (*Hyacinthus orientalis*)
Lily-of-the-valley (*Convallaria majalis*)
Narcissus (*Narcissus*)
Pansy (*Viola*)
Pasque flower (*Pulsatilla vulgaris*)
Periwinkle (*Vinca*)
Persian buttercup (*Ranunculus asiaticus*)
Pieris (*Pieris*)
Primula (*Primula* hybrids)
Snake's head fritillary (*Fritillaria meleagris*)
Solomon's seal (*Polygonatum* x *hybridum*)
Squill (*Scilla*)
Tulip (*Tulipa*)
Windflower (*Anemone*)

———— • ————

COLUMBINE
(*Aquilegia vulgaris*
'Nora Barlow')

ROSE
(*Rosa* 'New Dawn')

BUSY LIZZIE
(*Impatiens* New
Guinea hybrid)

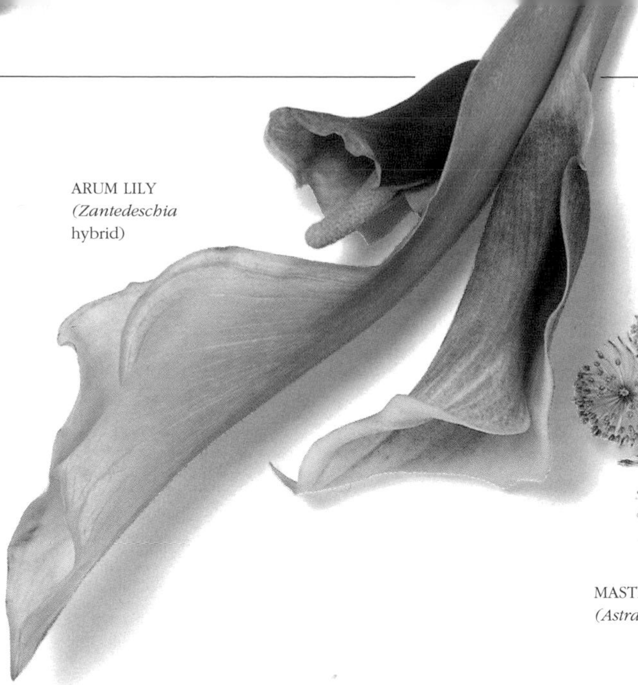

ARUM LILY
(Zantedeschia
hybrid)

MASTERWORT
(Astrantia major)

MEXICAN ORANGE
BLOSSOM
(Choisya ternata)

∽ SUMMER ∽

Arum lily *(Zantedeschia)*
Asparagus *(Asparagus)*
Astilbe *(Astilbe)*
Begonia *(Begonia)*
Bellflower *(Campanula)*
Bleeding heart *(Dicentra)*
Busy Lizzie *(Impatiens)*
Coleus *(Coleus blumei)*
Columbine *(Aquilegia)*
Common rue *(Ruta graveolens)*
Creeping fig *(Ficus pumila)*
Fuchsia *(Fuchsia)*
Heuchera *(Heuchera)*
Hosta *(Hosta)*
Japanese maple *(Acer palmatum)*
Lewisia *(Lewisia)*
Lily *(Lilium)*
Lobelia *(Lobelia)*
Loosestrife *(Lysimachia)*
Masterwort *(Astrantia)*
Monkey flower *(Mimulus)*
Pansy *(Viola)*
Pelargonium *(Pelargonium)*
Persian buttercup *(Ranunculus asiaticus)*
Pick-a-back plant *(Tolmiea menziesii)*
Plectranthus *(Plectranthus)*
Potentilla *(Potentilla)*
Rose *(Rosa)*
Scabious *(Scabiosa)*
Sweet alyssum *(Lobularia maritima)*
Tobacco plant *(Nicotiana)*
Wandering Jew *(Tradescantia)*
Yucca *(Yucca)*

———— • ————

∽ AUTUMN ∽

Chrysanthemum *(Chrysanthemum)*
Cotoneaster *(Cotoneaster)*
Cyclamen *(Cyclamen)*
Fuchsia *(Fuchsia)*
Heather *(Calluna)*
Houttuynia *(Houttuynia)*
Hydrangea *(Hydrangea)*
Japanese maple *(Acer palmatum)*
Michaelmas daisy *(Aster)*
Pernettya *(Pernettya)*
Polygonum *(Polygonum)*

———— • ————

LILY
(Lilium 'La Reve')

HELLEBORE
(Helleborus x *sternii)*

TOBACCO PLANT
(Nicotiana alata
Sensation Series)

PANSY
(Viola x *wittrockiana)*

ASTILBE
(Astilbe x
arendsii)

SHADY POSITIONS

SHADY SITES are the most difficult for growing plants. There are plants that like shade, but the choice is limited. Several types of shade exist. The most problematic is deep shade, created by the overhead shadows of dense trees or a roof. Shade from buildings can be a nuisance, but if the level of reflected light is high, there are many plants that will grow well there.

DEGREES OF SHADE

In deeply shaded areas between houses, or where there is a light well and little sky is visible, the overall light level is low, and this again is a problem. The plants then receive very little natural light, and soon become weak, and straggly. They are also more prone to pests, diseases and fungal infections. Painting walls in white or another light colour helps considerably by increasing the amount of reflected light in the area.

❧ Several foliage plants will grow relatively happily in deep shade. Of the evergreens, try bergenia, box, elaeagnus, fatsia, gaultheria, ivy, holly, evergreen honeysuckle, mahonia, osmanthus, pachysandra, pieris, sarcococca, skimmia, yew, periwinkle, and ferns. A number of ferns are evergreen or semi-evergreen, holding their fronds through the winter. Among summer-flowering plants, begonias and busy Lizzies give a good show; tobacco plants and fuchsias make less flowering growth and are not quite as effective in very deep shade.

❧ The choice is much wider in light shade, where there is no sun but the level of light is reasonably high, such as in the dappled light of a tree with delicate foliage, or in a light area that is shaded by buildings. Plants suitable for deep shade, but also most of the spring bulbs, and

HANGING COLOUR
Hanging baskets of fuchsias (ABOVE), suspended from the branches of a deciduous tree, thrive in its light shade.

SERENE GREENS
A shady terrace (LEFT) furnished with bowls of ferns, asparagus, variegated-leaved fuchsia, tobacco plants, ivy, and hostas. Even the bay tree grows in a tub.

shrubs, flowering perennials and annuals, such as bellflowers, lobelias, cranesbill, and pansies, will grow in such a spot. Among the shrubs, aucuba, bamboo, camellia, Mexican orange blossom, hydrangea, cherry laurel, and viburnum will flourish in such a position.

FOCUS ON FOLIAGE

Few flowering plants are suitable for containers in shade, so it is as well to concentrate on foliage plantings, and add small amounts of seasonal colour.

❧ The golden elaeagnus, euonymus, and Mexican orange blossom all make a darkish area seem much brighter, almost as if the sun were shining. Sadly, the silver-leaved plants do not do well without some sunshine.

❧ There are also the plants with bold-shaped or coloured foliage, such as fatsia and bamboo, and the bronze-leaved heuchera 'Palace Purple'. Ferns all do tremendously well if you give them a potting mixture with some leafmould added. Some, such as polystichum, blechnum, and phyllitis, are both hardy and evergreen. In temperate climates, holly fern, tree fern, maidenhair, stag horn fern, woodwardias, and the silver-leaved phlebodium all grow magnificently in pots. Aspidistras also do very well in the deepest shade, as long as the temperature does not fall much below freezing.

❧ I am always surprised by what will grow well in a shady part of my garden in London. Aspidistra, clivia, New Zealand ferns, a Chusan palm, and even an epiphyllum cactus have all lived outside for many years. I even have photographs of the cactus in full flower, surrounded and partially covered by snow in mid winter. So do not be disheartened by your shady patch. There are bound to be some treasures that will flourish there.

SHADY RETREAT

POSITIONED JUST OUTSIDE THE KITCHEN, this area is paved to provide an outside dining room for the warm summer months. I always believe that an eating area should be relatively shady: nothing is more unpleasant than sitting at the garden table with plates of melting butter, wilting salad, and oily cheese, blasted by the sun.

✗ This terrace is paved in red brick paviours and sheltered by a lush, 2.7m- (9ft-) high, yew hedge, planted in a U-shape. Its only permanent plant features are six pots of box, clipped in a variety of formal shapes, and rectangular beds edged with low-growing box and filled, this year, with white busy Lizzies. A cool, green place in winter, it can be given a totally different feel in summer, with a few large pots of flowering plants in various colour schemes.

✗ The colour of the brick paviours prompted this choice of rich reds, with bright and pale pinks. The yellows were a happy accident – they should have been pale pink!

Box *(Buxus sempervirens)*
A tough shrub that thrives in almost any condition, and can be clipped into interesting shapes.

Tuberous begonia
(Begonia x tuberhybrida)
Watch out for mildew.

Terracotta pots
A mixture of large, round, and square, handmade terracotta pots, ranging in size from 45-55cm (18-22in) in diameter.

Tobacco plant
(Nicotiana 'Pink Bedder')
Cut back by about 15cm (6in) after the first flush of flowers to promote side shoots and new flowering growths.

Pendulous tuberous begonia *(Begonia x tuberhybrida pendula)*
Forms a waterfall of colour all summer long, and up until the first frosts.

Although plants grown in shade need less water than those placed in sunshine, it is still vital that you keep the potting mixture just moist, never soggy, and give them a weekly feed of liquid fertilizer. Woodland is the natural habitat of most shade lovers, so generally they grow best in a rich potting mixture. Since plants growing in shade are not as healthy as those in other sites, they are more susceptible to pests and diseases.

Fuchsia (*Fuchsia* 'Thalia')
A fast-growing, deciduous variety with an upright habit and long, slender, dark orange flowers, accented by bronzy green foliage.

SCHEMES FOR SHADE

FOR A SHADY GARDEN, green has to be the predominant colour. Cool, but at the same time welcoming, it feels just right for sites that the sun does not reach. Plenty of shrubs grow happily in shade, although you must take into account the degree of shade when making your choice. Hardly any plants grow in very dense shade, where the light is extremely low, but moderate shade is not a problem. Among the evergreens, box, yew, and hemlock all survive and can be clipped into dramatic shapes. Aucuba, bamboo, Mexican orange blossom, holly, privet, and mahonia, also evergreens, will grow into good-sized specimens in large containers. For bright shade, where there is plenty of reflected light, rhododendrons and camellias can produce a display of showy flowers. Most of these shrubs look best planted as single specimens, surrounded by trailing plants, such as small-leaved ivies and periwinkle.

POOLS OF COLOUR

Against this background of greenery, you can add containers of seasonal colour. Tuberous begonias, busy Lizzies, fuchsias, and tobacco plants all combine well together, and their colours show up vibrantly against green foliage. I find that two or three of the small-flowered, pendulous begonias look most effective in a low bowl or pot on the end of a low wall.

✗ For colour in spring in a shady site, try planting bulbs. They will flower well in containers in a shady place for at least one season. In winter, plantings of box, euonymus, and ivy thrive in shady positions. If your garden is not too cold, you could also try growing winter cherry, which has orange-red fruit, with evergreen skimmia or leucothöe.

Indoor Plants
✗ An evergreen planting for a shady doorway (ABOVE), consisting mainly of plants traditionally grown in the house. In the summer months, spider plant (*Chlorophytum comosum*), pick-a-back plant (*Tolmiea menziesii*), and the grass *Pogonatherum paniceum* all grow well outdoors.

Victorian Plant Stand
✗ A wrought-iron plant stand (RIGHT) holds pots of shade-loving maidenhair ferns (*Adiantum capillus-veneris*), busy Lizzies (*Impatiens*), creeping fig (*Ficus pumila*), and begonias (*Begonia* 'Elatior hybrid'). Asters prefer semi-shade, but once they have buds, you can move them into shade for blooming.

PLANTS FOR SHADE

A MULTITUDE OF SHADE-LOVING, evergreen shrubs and perennials grow extremely well in containers. Their main attraction is their foliage, which comes in a wide range of shapes and colours and which is particularly welcome in winter, when deciduous plants are bare. But you are by no means limited to foliage-only plants for containers in the shade. In spring there are bulbs, most of which grow well in a shady but light position, for at least one season. Other possibilities include sweet-scented lily-of-the-valley, pansies, and primulas.

Come the summer, some of the most brilliantly coloured flowers – begonias, fuchsias, tobacco plants, and busy Lizzies, as well as lilies and bellflowers – are happiest in shade with a reasonable light level. All of these flowers look stunning next to ferns and hostas. Nearly every house plant also thrives in a bright but shaded position outdoors in summer.

HONEYSUCKLE
(*Lonicera japonica* 'Halliana')

BEGONIA
(*Begonia* x *tuberhybrida*)

FERN
(*Osmunda regalis*)

⁓ WINTER ⁓

Aucuba (*Aucuba*)
Bamboos
Bergenia (*Bergenia*)
Box (*Buxus*)
Conifers
Evergreen ferns
Fatsia (*Fatsia*)
Gaultheria (*Gaultheria*)
Hellebore (*Helleborus niger*)
Ivy (*Hedera helix*)
Leucothöe (*Leucothöe*)
Mahonia (*Mahonia*)
Pachysandra (*Pachysandra*)
Pansy (*Viola*)
Skimmia (*Skimmia*)

———— • ————

Most of the plants recommended for winter are evergreens, and therefore provide year-round interest.

⁓ SPRING ⁓

Azalea/rhododendron (*Rhododendron*)
Bergenia (*Bergenia*)
Camellia (*Camellia*)
Dog's tooth violet (*Erythronium*)
Hellebore (*Helleborus*)
Lily-of-the-valley (*Convallaria majalis*)
Narcissus (*Narcissus*)
Pansy (*Viola*)
Periwinkle (*Vinca*)
Pieris (*Pieris*)
Primula (*Primula*)
Snake's head fritillary (*Fritillaria meleagris*)
Solomon's seal (*Polygonatum* x *hybridum*)
Tulip (*Tulipa*)

———— • ————

RHODODENDRON
(*Rhododendron* 'Nobleanum')

HOSTA
(*Hosta sieboldiana*)

BEGONIA
(*Begonia* x *tuberhybrida*)

PACHYSANDRA
(Pachysandra terminalis)

BEGONIA
(Begonia x
tuberhybrida)

JAPANESE SHIELD
FERN
*(Dryopteris
erythrosora)*

PHILODENDRON
(Philodendron)

IVY
*(Hedera helix
'Duck's Foot')*

∾ Summer ∾

Begonia *(Begonia)*
Bellflower *(Campanula)*
Busy Lizzie *(Impatiens)*
Creeping fig *(Ficus pumila)*
Ferns
Fuchsia *(Fuchsia)*
Honeysuckle *(Lonicera)*
Hosta *(Hosta)*
Jasmine *(Jasminum)*
Monkey flower *(Mimulus)*
Pansy *(Viola)*
Philodendron *(Philodendron)*
Pick-a-back plant *(Tolmiea menziesii)*
Tobacco plant *(Nicotiana)*

───── • ─────

∾ Autumn ∾

Begonia *(Begonia)*
Cyclamen *(Cyclamen)*
Elaeagnus *(Elaeagnus ebbingei)*
Fuchsia *(Fuchsia)*
Hydrangea *(Hydrangea)*
Japanese anemone *(Anemone* x *hybrida)*
Kirengeshoma *(Kirengeshoma palmata)*
Maple *(Acer)*
Pyracantha *(Pyracantha)*
St John's wort *(Hypericum)*

───── • ─────

MAHONIA
*(Mahonia
lomariifolia)*

LILY-OF-THE-VALLEY
(Convallaria majalis)

HYDRANGEA
(Hydrangea macrophylla)

FATSIA
*(Fatsia
japonica)*

EXPOSED POSITIONS

AN EXPOSED GARDEN is one that is subjected to extremes of weather: strong winds, harsh sun, and cold, either separately or in combination. Roof terraces, often blasted by both wind and sun, are perfect examples of exposed sites, so too are gardens on unsheltered hillsides, flat, open expanses, or city plots at the end of a man-made wind tunnel.

✂ Growing any plants in containers under such conditions is not easy. Indeed a combination of wind, sun, and extreme cold can be pretty lethal. Plants in pots dry out extremely quickly, and their leaves and flowers may become wind-browned, even if they have been well watered. It pays to give them a reasonable depth of potting mixture: the shallower the container, the quicker the soil dries out. And if using small containers, choose ones made from non-porous materials, such as plastic or fibreglass, that retain as much moisture as possible.

—— PROTECTION ——

It makes sense to take advantage of any protection that is available on the site. Position your tubs beside walls, ballustrading, or the sides of balconies and fences – all these features help to break up the force of the wind and provide shelter from strong sun or rain.

✂ Many of the taller, large-leaved plants or shrubs and trees, such as bamboo, with very flexible stems (SEE PAGES 132-3), tolerate both sun and wind, and are useful for giving protection to more delicate specimens. When using these larger plants on a roof terrace or balcony, make sure that the structure is strong enough to hold them. Do not underestimate the weight of large plants in

PRIME VIEW
To preserve this magnificent riverside view (ABOVE), the plantings of zonal pelargoniums, French marigolds, ivy, and coleus are kept low.

BULBS ON A BALCONY
Spring bulbs, pansies, box, and ivy (LEFT) are a good choice for adding colour to a wind-swept balcony.

good-sized tubs, pots, and troughs when filled with potting mixture, especially after a thorough watering.

—— TOUGH CHOICE ——

If you have an exposed garden, it is essential that you choose very tough plants for growing in your containers.

✂ Long stemmed plants hate being battered and whipped about by wind and rain. If you want to position containers in an area that is in a wind tunnel, perhaps between high buildings, or somewhere that is affected by coastal winds, choose plants that have strong, tough, or wiry stems, and trim straggly growth.

✂ It is worth remembering that low-growing plants either miss the worst of high winds or they are strong enough to withstand them. Plant them in a sink or a low trough to give year-round interest (SEE PAGES 90-1). Although alpines tolerate both sun and wind exposure in summer, they dislike a combination of cold, icy winds and damp in winter, so it may be necessary to give them some form of overhead shelter, such as a sheet of glass.

—— SEASONAL COLOUR ——

All of the popular spring bulbs, especially the low-growing species and varieties, flower in exposed sites. If you are growing groups of them in a windy position, stake them well when they are only a few centimetres high to prevent the leaves and flower stems from breaking in strong winds. Once they have finished flowering, and all possibility of frost has passed, you can replace the bulbs with summer-flowering annuals, many of which will tolerate lots of sun at a time of year when high winds are not usually such a problem.

ROOF TOP OF TREES

BLASTED BY THE SUN and battered by the wind, roof gardens are prime examples of exposed sites. They are not the best places to grow garden plants, but if you live in a city apartment, a roof terrace can make a useful, extra room, bringing greenery closer to the urban home and providing a pleasant and relaxing place to sit, with the sky as a ceiling.

— WEIGHT CONSIDERATIONS —

The large size and sturdy structure of this roof terrace, at the top of an apartment block, makes it possible to grow a selection of heavy specimen trees in pots. The owners checked with an architect how much weight the roof could take, as large containers can be very heavy, especially when they are wet. Usually, it is best to place heavy containers near load-bearing walls, rather than arrange them in the middle of the terrace where the roof is unlikely to be supported.

—— POTTED TREES ——

Provided they are watered and fed well, trees and large shrubs grow well in good-sized containers, even in exposed positions. Generally, pots measuring 1m (36in) across will take a 3.6m- (12ft-) high tree, although in exposed sites it is best to choose species that are not higher than 3m (10ft). Unless they are well anchored, they may blow over in high winds.

※ When it comes to selecting trees, it is best not to consider fast-growing species, such as eucalyptus and ailanthus – they will soon grow too big for their tubs. Conifers do well, if they are watered frequently, although just a short spell without sufficient moisture kills them. For exposed spots, however, pines and junipers are the most suitable conifers – high winds will brown the foliage of other species.

Locust *(Gleditsia triacanthos* 'Sunburst') Grown for its foliage, which retains its golden colour all summer.

Cordyline *(Cordyline australis)* An attractive evergreen with a dramatic architectural shape.

Mountain pine *(Pinus mugo)* An extremely tough conifer, which grows into a good shape.

Sweet bay *(Laurus nobilis)* Only grow in mild areas, as frost can kill it in winter.

PLANT CARE

In an exposed site, plants in pots need frequent watering because of the drying effects of the wind and sun. Even in winter, you should water them, except when the temperature is below freezing. Spray the leaves of large, newly planted specimens frequently, but avoid doing so in hot sunlight. After their first year, underwater rather than overwater them.

Variegated maple (*Acer negundo* 'Variegatum') Distinguished by its pretty pinky-cream and green-striped leaves.

Spruce (*Picea glauca albertiana* 'Conica') Grows into a perfect pyramid of dense, bright green foliage.

Sacred bamboo (*Nandina domestica*) A species that needs a sunny position, but also the protection of other plants to keep it sheltered from the wind.

Black bamboo (*Phyllostachys nigra*) A frost-hardy variety with beautiful, evergreen leaves. In their second season, the stems turn black.

Juniper (*Juniperus sabina* 'Tamariscifolia') A tough conifer, with a low, spreading habit.

Flax (*Phormium cookianum* 'Variegatum') Grown for its decorative, strap-like, evergreen leaves.

SCHEMES FOR EXPOSED POSITIONS

IN GARDENS subjected to strong wind, sun, and cold, only certain types of plants will grow well. Generally, it is advisable to choose low-growing plants, as they miss the worst of high winds. Plan a permanent planting based on tough-stemmed shrubs, such as cotoneasters, spreading conifers, elaeagnus, euonymus, and potentillas. To this you can then add summer colour with annuals, such as zonal pelargoniums, snapdragons, marigolds, nasturtiums, and verbena, all of which cope in windy situations and also thrive in strong sun, provided you do not allow the soil to become too dry. In hot, summer weather on a sunny roof garden or terrace, this probably means watering twice or maybe even three times a day.

In a cold, windy site, check which plants are hardy in your neighbours' gardens before buying winter evergreens. Most spring bulbs are fairly tough and look good planted around shrubs. Plant out low-growing, summer annuals once the risk of frost has passed.

Drought Resistance

Rock plants and succulents do not mind being baked by the sun or lashed by the wind, although they do object to too much wet, especially in winter. Many of them have evergreen foliage so they remain decorative throughout the year. A single planting of stonecrop *(Sedum obtusatum)* grows informally in a low stone bowl (LEFT). The rough-hewn pedestal that supports the stone bowl rises from a bright clump of lavender *(Lavandula angustifolia)*. Low-growing lavenders, with their tight mounds of foliage, covered with a haze of flowers for many weeks in summer, are ideal for exposed gardens.

For Sun and Wind

Low-growing and prostrate plants (RIGHT) – helichrysum, lobelia, floss flower, verbena, scabious, bellflower, and monkey flower – survive exposure to hot sun well. They need to be watered, but they will not require as much attention as the more delicate and taller plants. Bear in mind that the types of plants that grow on rocky hillsides around the Mediterranean, such as thymes, sages, and many silver-leaved species, suit sunny, exposed sites.

PLANTS FOR EXPOSED SITES

AN EXPOSED SITE is not the easiest place to grow plants in containers. While gardening in such a site is a challenge, there are a sufficient number of plants you can use that can make this type of container garden look attractive for most, if not all, of the year. Remember, that plants which are closely related to wild flowers growing in difficult situations are the most likely to succeed in exposed sites. A large number of tough, aromatic plants – especially those with silver foliage – succulents, and strap-leaved plants, such as cordylines and yuccas, will also grow well.

ZONAL PELARGONIUM
(*Pelargonium* 'Rio')

ZONAL PELARGONIUM
(*Pelargonium* 'Yale')

BEDDING DAHLIA
(*Dahlia* 'Fascination')

WALLFLOWER
(*Cheiranthus*
'Rufus')

ᔰ WINTER ᔰ

Bay (*Laurus*) s
Bayberry (*Myrica pensylvanica*) WSC
Blueberry (*Vaccinium*) WC
Box (*Buxus*) WSD
Cotoneaster (*Cotoneaster*) WSC
Cypress (*Cupressus arizonica* and
C. *macrocarpa*) WS
Elaeagnus (*Elaeagnus*) WS
Euonymus (*Euonymus fortunei*) WCD
Euonymus (*Euonymus japonicus*) WD
Gorse (*Ulex*) WS
Holly (*Ilex*) WS
Juniper (*Juniperus*) WSC
Lavender (*Lavandula*) WS
Pachysandra (*Pachysandra*) WC
Pieris (*Pieris floribunda*) W
Pine (*Pinus*) WSC
Rosemary (*Rosmarinus*) WS
Sage (*Salvia officinalis*) WS
Southernwood (*Artemisia*) WS

Most of the plants recommended for winter are evergreens, and therefore provide year-round interest.

ᔰ SPRING ᔰ

Aubretia (*Aubretia*) WSC
Bugle (*Ajuga*) WC
Crocus (*Crocus*) WSC
Gorse (*Ulex*) WS
Grape hyacinth (*Muscari*) WSCD
Hyacinth (*Hyacinthus*) WSC
Iberis (*Iberis*) SD
Iris (*Iris*) WSC
Lower-growing daffodils (*Narcissus*) WSC
Lower-growing narcissi (*Narcissus*) WSC
Lower-growing tulips (*Tulipa*) WSC
Pansy (*Viola*) WS
Puschkinia (*Puschkinia*) WSCD
Saxifrage (*Saxifraga*) WS
Spurge (*Euphorbia*) WS
Squill (*Scilla*) WSC
Wallflower (*Cheiranthus*) WSC

ᔰ KEY ᔰ

W tolerates wind
S tolerates sun
C tolerates cold to –33˚C (–20˚F)
D tolerates drought

AMARANTHUS
(*Amaranthus caudatus*)

NASTURTIUM (*Tropaeolum
majus* 'Alaska')

ACHILLEA (*Achillea
millefolium*)

SCABIOUS (*Scabiosa
atropurpurea* 'Cockade')

EUONYMUS
(Euonymus
fortunei
'Sunspot')

STATICE
(Limonium sinuatum)

PHLOMIS
(Phlomis italica)

TULIP (Tulipa
'Garden Party')

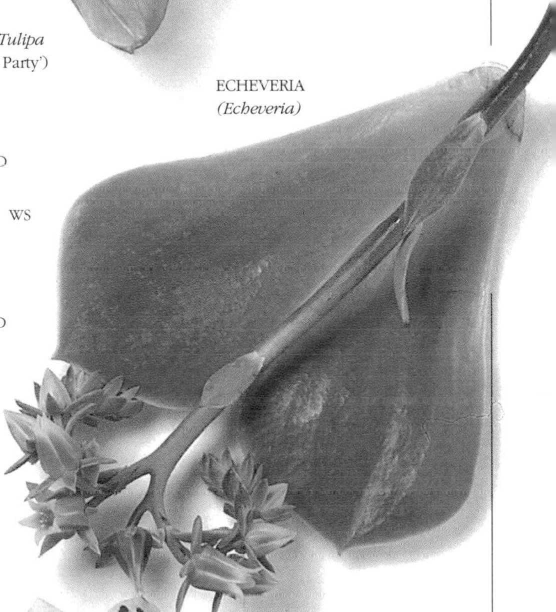

ECHEVERIA
(Echeveria)

～ SUMMER ～

Achillea (Achillea) WSC
Agave (Agave) WS
Aloe (Aloe) WD
Bergamot (Monarda) WS
Cordyline (Cordyline) S
Cornflower (Centaurea) WS
Echeveria (Echeveria) WS
Houseleek (Sempervivum) WSC
Livingstone daisy (Mesembryanthemum) WSD
Locust (Gleditsia) WSD
Maple (Acer) WC
Marigold (Calendula/Tagetes) WS
Nasturtium (Tropaeolum) WS
New Zealand flax (Phormium) WS
Pelargonium (Pelargonium) WS
Petunia (Petunia) S
Phlomis (Phlomis) WS
Pink (Dianthus) WS
Portulaca (Portulaca) WS
Scabious (Scabiosa) WSC
Snapdragon (Antirrhinum) WS
Statice (Limonium) WS
Valerian (Centranthus) WS
Yucca (Yucca) WSD

———— • ————

～ AUTUMN ～

Amaranthus (Amaranthus) S
Autumn crocus (Colchicum) WSCD
Ceratostigma (Ceratostigma) WS
Chrysanthemum (Chrysanthemum) WS
Cotinus (Cotinus) WS
Dahlia (Dahlia) WS
Helenium (Helenium) WSC
Ice plant (Sedum spectabile) WSCD
Kaffir lily (Schizostylis) WS
Liriope (Liriope) WSD
Nerine (Nerine bowdenii) WS
Stonecrop (Sedum) WSCD
Sumach (Rhus) WSC

———— • ————

EUONYMUS
(Euonymus fortunei
'Silver Queen')

PINK (Dianthus
'Monica Wyatt')

SNAPDRAGON
(Antirrhinum majus)

$\mathscr{S}$PECIFIC LOCATIONS

MOST PLACES in the garden are improved by a plant, or group of plants, grown in an attractive container. Often, the restricting factor is how many plants you can manage to water without it becoming too much of a chore. Give priority to sites that are constantly in view, or near the house. If the side walls of the building can be drilled safely, secure attractive wall baskets, hayracks, and hanging baskets to them, ideally near doorways, or above paths where they can be enjoyed, as well as easily watered and looked after.

—— PRIDE OF PLACE ——

Doorways are very important places, especially the front door where plants should be welcoming. The plants need not be tall or expensive specimens. Front doors often have steps leading to them, and a tiered array of plant-filled pots sitting on the steps will give an informal welcome. Elsewhere in the garden, a flight of steps, or maybe just a single step, can be brought to life with a pot overflowing with trailing plants.

If you are fortunate enough to have a porch, deck, or verandah running along a side of your house, this makes a perfect place for some groups of containers. Use weathered terracotta, stone, or wood containers that will blend well with the walls and flooring of these structures. If you want to protect the floors, use plant-pot saucers.

—— THE UNEXPECTED ——

It is always a pleasant surprise to come across container plantings unexpectedly: to turn a corner and see a path bounded by pots of colourful annuals or more subdued, clipped box trees; to

WARM WELCOME
Simple pots of regal pelargoniums (ABOVE) and echevarias have a cottagey look that makes this imposing house entrance homely and welcoming.

A FORMAL SETTING
Hydrangea appears simple, cool and elegant planted in formal planter (LEFT) against a thuja hedge at the end of a gravel path edged with clipped box.

walk through a dense screen of shrubs and find a comfortable seat beside a quiet pool, surrounded by pots of blue African lilies or plumbago; to walk out of the kitchen door and find yourself among a host of pots filled with aromatic, culinary herbs; to suddenly notice a small window box discreetly perched on the ledge of an old, ivy-covered brick wall, in cool shade.

—— FOCAL POINT ——

Search out the special places in your garden, where an imposing pot or urn could be used as a focal point. It might be at the end of a long, straight path against a formal evergreen hedge, or opposite a door from the house, or a large window overlooking a paved patio or terrace. Like statues, containers are important garden ornaments and their plantings need to be carefully considered so that they will both stand out and relate well to the surrounding planting schemes. Sometimes a simple planting of just one type of plant, species, or variety may well be the answer, especially if the container, itself, is strongly architectural or highly decorative.

—— PRACTICAL CONSIDERATIONS ——

Make sure that a tap or source of water is never too far away from the site you choose for containers. It is all too easy to give up on plants if you have to carry a watering can a long way, particularly in hot weather when they need watering most frequently. Nothing looks sadder than a neglected pot of plants. But then nothing looks better than a group of pots, or even just a simple, single urn, tub, or window box, positioned in the right place, and planted with an eye-catching scheme.

PORCHES AND PERGOLAS

PORCHES CAN BE SIMPLE, as a covered but open structure sheltering the approach to a doorway, or they can be much grander, with a roof and sides attached to the house. Being sheltered, they are useful places to grow favourite plants, which may not tolerate the cold, wet, or wind. If container plants are under the roof, you will need to water them carefully.

❧ Pergolas usually consist of a series of pillars made from stone, brick, or iron, supporting a top frame, ideally covered by climbing plants. They may be freestanding and cover an outdoor eating area, or they may form part of a paved walk. Alternatively they can be built with one side attached to a building, like a verandah, and without an enclosed roof.

❧ As such, pergolas do not offer the same degree of protection to container plants as porches. They do, however, benefit from being furnished with pot plants, particularly around the base of the columns where climbing plants tend to become thin and woody. Some scented plants are a must. In spring, grow plenty of scented narcissi and hyacinths for the first sorties into the garden. In summer, try marvel of Peru, or angels' trumpets, a robust but frost-tender shrub, which has hanging white trumpets, renowned for their delicious, evening fragrance in summer and autumn. Also add pots of different lilies, carefully chosen to span the summer.

PERFECT PROPORTIONS

The proportions of standards and mop-heads make them ideal for standing against the pillars of a pergola: use flowering pelargoniums and fuchsias in summer, and hardy evergreens in winter. Bay is a strong-growing pot plant that can be trained into miniature columns, pyramids, and trees. It is easy to care for, but only moderately hardy, and does not like very cold winds.

❧ If you want to cover a pergola with climbers, avoid growing them in pots, as they are unlikely to grow big enough to do a good job. If possible, it is better to plant them in the open ground.

Grandiose Porch
❧ An assortment of pots (LEFT), planted with the cranesbill, *Geranium palmatum*, rain daisies, verbena, heliotrope, helichrysum, salvia, and agrostemma, furnish an old stone porch. They give a wild and informal look to this grand entrance area making it more inviting: a place to sit and relax with a book on a hot and lazy summer's afternoon.

Pergola Planting
❧ A contemporary pergola made from cedar beams, supported by brick columns (RIGHT). As it is sheltered, this is an ideal site for growing a standard fuchsia and regal perlargoniums, whose blooms can be damaged by rain. To prevent standards from blowing over, secure them between the brick columns with wire.

FLIGHTS OF STEPS

AKE MORE OF A FEATURE OF STEPS in your garden, and soften the edges of paving surfaces, by placing pots at the sides. Leave enough room to walk up the steps comfortably, although, if you are growing aromatic plants, it is an added bonus to brush against their foliage, releasing the fragrance as you walk past. I always grow a pot of lemon verbena at the base of some sunny steps in my garden – its leaves exude the most delicious, lemon scent, which makes walking up the steps a sheer delight. Generally, I find that low, sprawling plants look most effective on steps: a pot planted with ivy-leaved pelargoniums, trailing lobelia, some portulacas, or nasturtiums works well.

⚘ Choose containers that will stand firm and steady on the treads and will complement the fabric of the steps. Well-weathered terracotta looks attractive on almost any type of hard surface: brick, stone, concrete, metal, or wood. Glazed and coloured pots need to be used with more care. They seem most effective on the more hard-surfaced steps, such as those made from tile, stones, and concrete. However, there are no rules. Sometimes the most unexpected combinations work to perfection.

Scented Stairway

⚘ A simple pot (RIGHT) of tobacco plants (*Nicotiana alata*) sits comfortably in the curve of this shady, iron stairway, leading from the house down to the garden. Planted in early summer, tobacco plants will flower through the summer until the first frosts, exuding a delicious, nutmeg-like scent from dusk till dawn. The stairs are next to a paved area – it is always a pleasure to have scented flowers near to where you relax on summer evenings.

A Complement to Old Stone

⚘ The clusters of weathered, terracotta pots (BELOW) on each side of this shallow flight of steps give a great sense of perspective. Situated on the sunny side of the building, the site is just right for ivy-leaved and zonal pelargoniums, which flower in summer and autumn, demanding only minimum attention. The pale pink flowers set off the grey stone steps and old, wooden door especially well.

DOORWAYS

OORWAYS give both a first and a last impression of your house. The plants around them – often grown in containers as there is little or no soil on the site – should create a feeling of simple ease and beauty that makes visitors sense that all is well.

A planting for a doorway requires careful consideration. Both containers and plants need to suit the area in scale, colour, and texture. Terracotta and stone – my favourite materials – are a safe choice as they enhance most situations. Stone is expensive, but reconstituted stone soon looks as good when well weathered.

—— STANDARD WELCOME ——

Tall plants, especially standards, set off a doorway well. Mop-headed bays are great favourites, but privets and some conifers (SEE PAGE 166) can be also trained into decorative shapes. In summer, standard pelargoniums are ideal for a sunny doorway and standard fuchsias grow well in a semi-shady or shady porch. A pair of standards, one on each side of the door, looks formal, but where there is not enough room for two plantings, a single tub is just as striking. Bays and conifers soon take up all the root room in their containers, leaving little space for additional plantings, but around the base of other standards you can introduce trailing ivy, spring bulbs, and annuals for seasonal variation.

—— FLIGHT OF STEPS ——

When wide steps lead up to a door, arrange pots with evergreen foliage and seasonal colour down the sides. If only a little space is available, a single pot of lavender is impressive in a sunny doorway, and fuchsias or hostas make a simple statement in shade. In all cases, the containers should be overflowing and opulent.

Shady Exit
A shady spot beside a door (ABOVE) is ideal for eustoma *(Eustoma grandiflorum)*, busy Lizzies *(Impatiens walleriana)*, fuchsias *(Fuchsia)*, fine-leaved maple *(Acer palmatum)*, ferns *(Polystichum setiferum)*, and tobacco plants *(Nicotiana alata)*.

Weathered Door
A simple planting (BELOW) of pale pink, daisy-like marguerites *(Argyranthemum* 'Mary Wootton') suits this sunny corner beside a weathered door. If regularly deadheaded, the marguerites should have several flushes of their pretty flowers.

Style and Symmetry
A period entrance (RIGHT) is perfect for a formal planting. Here, mop-headed privets *(Ligustrum vulgare* 'Buxifolium') grow with a seasonal planting of regal pelargoniums *(Pelargonium* 'Braque') and ivy *(Hedera helix* 'Sagittifolia Variegata').

WALLS AND FENCES

W HEN SPACE ON THE GROUND is at a premium, you can grow plants on or up, walls and fences. If the planting is above ground, the container must be firmly fixed in position, so that there is no possibility of it falling. Secure boxes on to window sills with a metal bracket or a strong wire restraint. Frequently check that the brackets and fittings remain both strong and secure.

Containers standing at the base of a wall will probably be quite visible, so the material from which they are made should relate well to the background. Terracotta, stone, and painted wood are good in almost all situations; unpainted wooden containers tend to look better against rustic buildings; and the smoother finishes of fibreglass, plastic, or metal are most effective in front of contemporary structures. You can have fibreglass containers, made to order, in almost any colour. Although they are quite expensive, the additional cost for a special colour is not that much extra.

As fences are not as strong as walls, you should only hang light containers, such as wire half baskets, on them. It is easy to make your own containers, using a double layer of chicken wire, cut to make a half or quarter sphere and stuffed with moss. Secure it to the fence with hooks and screws. If you have a fence crying out for foliage cover, but there is no bed at its base, use good-sized containers beside it. Tubs made from teak or cedar look extremely smart against wood. Plant them up with ivy or evergreen honeysuckle.

Coloured Backdrop

If you are unsure what colours look good together, choose a closely related range. Here, I have used red-based colours: pinks, reds, and white for a window box (BELOW) against a dusky pink wall.

Climbing Pelargoniums

In France, Germany, and Italy, pelargoniums are widely used in containers (RIGHT) because they grow so profusely during the warm summers. They are trained up walls, as well as left to trail.

GARDEN PATHS

PAVED AREAS CRY OUT for container plantings, and garden paths are no exception. Frequently, a path edges a border that is filled with beautiful colour for a month, but once the flowers die down, it looks quite dull. It is at this point that pots come into their own, extending the flowering season of an area by a few months. There is just one obvious consideration – make sure the path is wide enough to leave room for the containers and anyone wishing to walk down it.

DELIBERATE DISTRACTIONS

Another good reason for placing containers on a path is to slow any wanderers down on their journey and make them appreciate what lies along the way. It is all too easy to use a path simply as a means of getting from one place to another. Interesting plantings will slow you down as you pause to smell some fragrant leaves, to observe the way light falls on some flowers, or to admire intricate patterning on some foliage. Interestingly, if you line a path with two rows of identical pot plantings, it will soon become a quick walkway again. If a path is very wide, line pots down one side as a border, either with a permanent planting or with plants for seasonal colour.

MATCHING MATERIALS

Certain types of containers work especially well on certain surfaces. Terracotta is a natural choice for paths that are made from flag stones, bricks, or gravel. Reconstituted stone that has aged is also in keeping. Wooden containers, such as Versailles tubs, look particularly well against gravel, and the more rustic wooden barrels fit in perfectly with a bark path. In a woodland setting, try hollow trunks planted with ferns.

When you position the pots, bear in mind where the light is going to fall on the path, and site them so that the sun shines through the leaves on to the containers, creating dramatic or interesting shadows.

On the Bend
✗ A group of monkey flowers *(Mimulus aurantiacus)* growing in terracotta pots (ABOVE), brighten a bend in an old stone path with their sunny orange flowers that last from late spring until autumn.

Staggered Line
✗ The late afternoon light (LEFT) catches the leaves and flowers of this cheerful assortment of annual nasturtiums *(Tropaeolum)*, planted in old, oil jars from the south of France, and terracotta bowls.

Topiary
✗ A formal line of pyramid-shaped, clipped box *(Buxus sempervivens)* and mop-headed privet *(Ligustrum vulgare* 'Buxifolium'), divides the path from the lawn (RIGHT) and draws the eye – and the foot – to the far end of the route.

EVENING GARDEN

AFTER THE HEAT OF THE SUN HAS GONE, the garden seems to come alive with soft, sweet scents. It is a beautiful time of day to sit outside. If you have a paved eating area with chairs and a table, even if it is only a small terrace, a few pots of strongly scented plants are a must.

In dappled shade, a combination of lilies and tobacco plants can perfume the evening garden from early summer until mid autumn and make eating by lantern light the greatest of pleasures. Scented lilies are some of the most beautiful flowers. Their great, waxy trumpets open from gracefully pointed buds to pour forth waves of sweet, spicy perfume. It is impossible to judge which are the most beautiful. Madonna lilies, the earliest to open, have one of the clearest, sweetest fragrances, then come the regales and auratums, with scents reminiscent of nutmeg and vanilla, and finally, in late summer and early autumn, the speciosums, distinguished by reflexed petals and a soft, toffee-like perfume.

Among tobacco plants, the white-flowered forms have the strongest fragrance. They come into their own in the evening, when their flowers take on a new life, exuding a fragrance resembling sweet nutmeg. I favour the old-fashioned *Nicotiana alata*, easily raised from seed, as it has a better scent than most of the white bedders that you buy in trays. The taller, elegant, *Nicotiana sylvestris* flowers later in the summer and is also well scented.

Intoxicating Perfume

An iron staircase (LEFT) leading from the living room and kitchen to the garden terrace makes a perfect platform for stepped ranks of lilies, illuminated by lanterns holding candles. The regale lilies *(Lilium regale)*, seen here in high summer, are some of the easiest lilies to grow. Highly fragrant, they make ideal subjects for an evening garden as their white petals with pink reverses show up in the fading light. The lilies, 'Pink Perfection' and 'Golden Splendour', add just a hint of colour to the group.

White Flowers

Under a bower of vine leaves, and against a backdrop of cool, green ivy and camellia foliage (RIGHT), transluscent lilies 'La Reve' and 'Casa Blanca' and white busy Lizzies *(Impatiens walleriana)* grow in large terracotta pots. The heavily scented lily flowers last for several weeks. When a flower fades, remove it to encourage more buds to open. I chose pale flowers as they have a pure, luminescent quality in the fading light.

MAKING AND DECORATING CONTAINERS

❧

IT IS NOT ALWAYS NECESSARY to buy expensive pots. Vessels
you may have around the house can be adapted, or
you can make containers, using cheap materials.

IDEAS FOR IMPROVISATION
Lilies and ferns grow in pieces of tree stump and a bark pot.

PLANTING A BASKET

WITH THEIR NATURAL, RUSTIC LOOK, baskets make delightful containers for arrangements of small, summer-flowering annuals and trailing plants. Basketware tends to rot, especially in damp conditions, but you can increase its life span by painting it with an exterior wood preservative and lining the basket with a pot or a plastic bag. You must make drainage holes in the liner or the planting will drown. Use a basket with an open-weave base so that the water can drain away more freely, and the twigs will not rot so quickly.

1 Paint the basket with two coats of an exterior matt wood preservative, covering all the wood surfaces.

2 When the basket is dry, line it with a tough, black plastic bag. Trim it to size, and make holes in the base.

3 Fill with a rich, lightweight potting mixture. Try out the positioning, and plant up. Tuck any plastic out of sight.

Begonia (Begonia semperflorens) A popular bedding plant that can be raised from seed sown at the beginning of the year.

YOU WILL NEED
35cm- (14in-) long, oblong, open-weave twig basket
Exterior matt wood preservative
Paintbrush
Tough, black plastic bag, or plastic plant pot or low bowl
Scissors
Lightweight potting mixture of high nutritional value
Two ivies
Three begonias
Three white alyssum
Two floss flowers

Ivy (*Hedera helix* 'Gracilis')
Arrange to adorn the handle of this rustic basket.

Plant Positions

✄ Intended for a garden table (ABOVE), this basket is planted to be enjoyed from all angles. The white alyssum and ivy trail down the sides, while the mounds of begonia and floss flower fill the central area.

Summer Flowers

✄ This arrangement (LEFT) is best planted in early summer. It should flower well into the autumn and up to the first frosts, if watered plentifully, kept in a sunny position, and given a weekly liquid feed.

Floss flower (*Ageratum houstonianum* 'Blue Mink') Deadhead to encourage continuous flowering through the summer.

White alyssum (*Lobularia maritima* 'Little Dorrit') A compact form ideal for growing in a small basket.

155

CONVERTING A CHIMNEY POT

O LD CHIMNEY POTS, OR SECTIONS OF CERAMIC OR METAL PIPING, make original plant containers. As they take up less room than traditional pots and tubs, they are ideal for sites where space is limited: for example, on steps or balconies, in alleyways, or beside doorways. They are also useful for introducing height to a group of containers, as their elongated form provides the means to lift a planting well above the ground. The most effective plantings for chimney pots are those that form a mop-headed shape, or medium-height or low arrangements with foliage and flowers overflowing informally down the sides. Tall, narrow plants look unbalanced and out of scale with the base.

There are two ways of planting up chimney pots or pipes. The simplest technique is to fit a plastic pot exactly into the chimney pot top, so its lip is suspended on the rim of the chimney pot. As the plastic pot will need to be small, the size of the plants that you can grow is limited. The other technique is to make a base for the chimney pot so that, in effect, it becomes a very tall flower pot.

1 *Make the base. Line a saucer with newspaper and place a bottle top or cork, 2-2.5cm (¾-1in) in diameter and at least 2.5cm (1in) tall, in the centre where you want the drainage hole.*

2 *Clean the inside of the chimney pot with a mild disinfectant. Place it on the plastic saucer. Pour in enough ready-mix concrete to fill to 2cm (¾in) deep, holding the bottle top in place with a stick.*

3 *Spread the concrete evenly over the base of the chimney pot and leave, undisturbed, to set and dry. Invert the pot, remove the paper, and carefully knock out the bottle top to leave a drainage hole.*

Lobelia (*Lobelia erinus* 'White Cascade')
The trailing habit of lobelia breaks and softens the strong lines of the chimney-pot rim. Lobelia flowers for one season.

4 *Stand the pot upright for planting. Place a good layer of drainage material in the bottom of the pot, and then firm in a potting mixture of high nutritional value, with some peat added. Plant in early summer.*

Fuchsia (*Fuchsia* 'Annabel')
A tender shrub which flowers year after year if you keep it in a frost-free place over the winter.

YOU WILL NEED

Plastic plant pot saucer
Newspaper
Bottle top or cork
Old chimney pot
Mild disinfectant
Ready-mix concrete
Stick
Crocks
Potting mixture of high nutritional value
Peat
Four fuchsias
Four lobelias

Sprays of White

This fuchsia, with its arching sprays of white, dangling flowers, makes an excellent planting choice for this old clay chimney pot. Flowering for most of the summer and autumn, the fuchsia is complemented by the tiny white blooms of the lobelia. This arrangement is ideal for a semi-shady or even a shady site. Give the planting a mild liquid feed once a week for a long season of cool, white blooms.

Distressed chimney pot
The outside of this old chimney pot is deliberately not scrubbed to give it a weathered appearance.

DISGUISING A SINK

STONE SINKS ARE DIFFICULT TO FIND, and they are expensive to buy when you do track one down, but the old porcelain models are more readily available at not such extortionate prices. It is then quite easy to convert one into a good replica of a stone sink, by cleaning it, coating it with a contact bonding adhesive, and then applying a roughened layer of cement, sand, and peat, mixed together with water. The mixture should only take a few hours to dry thoroughly.

Once filled with soil and rocks, the sink will be immensely heavy, so place it in its final home while it is still empty. Even empty, it will be very heavy. (For details on how to move weighty containers, SEE PAGE 85.) If you intend to plant the sink with alpines, put it in a dry, sunny position and raise it on bricks or some pieces of stone, so the plug hole is well clear of the ground. As the roots of alpines dislike the wet, cover the bottom of the sink with a very thick layer of drainage crocks or pebbles, and fill it using a potting mixture which has a high gravel content. Coat the outside of the sink with live yoghurt and it should soon weather to resemble an old stone sink.

Stonecrop
(Sedum spurium 'Tricolor')
A hardy, mat-forming perennial.

Alpine poppy
(Papaver burseri)
A species that seeds itself from year to year.

Saxifrage *(Saxifraga paniculata)*
Clusters of rosettes produce airy spires of white flowers.

Poppy *(Papaver miyabeanum)*
The pale yellow flowers appear all summer. This poppy dislikes the winter wet.

1 *Thoroughly clean the outside and inside of the sink so that it is free of dirt and grease. Apply an even layer of contact adhesive to the outside surface and the top 5cm (2in) of the inside surface.*

2 *When the glue is tacky, apply a 1cm- (³/8in-) thick layer of cement mixed with sand and peat. Smooth on firmly with a trowel and roughen with a paintbrush.*

3 *Place the sink in its final position, and raise it off the ground with bricks or stones so that it can drain freely. Cover the base with a thick layer of crocks for good drainage. Fill the sink with potting mixture and fine gravel.*

4 *Arrange tufa over about a quarter of the surface area of the soil, leaving sufficient room for all the plants. Using an old screwdriver, chisel out holes in the rocks for stonecrops and houseleeks.*

YOU WILL NEED

Ceramic sink
Contact bonding adhesive
Application comb
Cement, sand, and peat (proportions 8:2:1)
Trowel
Stubby, old paintbrush
Crocks
Potting mixture of medium nutritional value, with fine gravel (proportions 4:1)
Tufa or porous rock
Large, old screwdriver

Common stonecrop (*Sedum acre*)
Fast growing, it has yellow flowers in the summer.

Alpine Conditions
⚒ Alpines like a sunny site, and soil which is on the dry side, so water sparingly. If your winters are wet, shelter the plants from rain with a sheet of glass.

Careful Planning
⚒ I placed the trailing sedums near the edges so that they spill over the rim, and jammed the rosette-forming succulents in the tufa. A saxifrage has its own corner in the trough, where it sits comfortably and neatly.

Lewisia (*Lewisia* Cotyledon hybrids)
Delicate blooms come in apricot, pink, and purple. The decorative rosettes of toothed leaves are evergreen.

Fairy thimbles (*Campanula cochleariifolia*)
A pretty, spreading perennial that flowers in the summer.

Saxifrage (*Saxifraga longifolia*)
This species produces large, arching pyramids of white flowers.

Stonecrop (*Sedum spathulifolium* 'Cape Blanco')
Silvery pink leaves and yellow flowers make a strong colour contrast.

USING AN OLD MOP BUCKET

WHEN A METAL MOP BUCKET springs a leak, bringing to an end its value in the kitchen, give it a second life in the garden by filling it with summer-flowering plants. Annuals will happily send their roots through the colander part of the bucket, where you wring out the mop, but larger plants are not suitable. You will need to drill holes in the base to provide drainage, as leak gaps are rarely sufficient.

Several other types of metal container can also be converted. Antique coppers, for example, are handsome-looking, although they are not easy to find and have become expensive to buy. Once kept outside, these soon lose their gleam, taking on a rich, dark patina. They are long-lasting and unaffected by frost. Milk churns, cream bowls, large tins, and even saucepans and fish kettles, can all be put to use in the garden, if you drill drainage holes in the bottom. They look most effective in an informal setting, used with building materials such as wood, old brick, and stone, or try standing them among low plants in a mixed border.

1 *Make five, evenly spaced, drainage holes in the bottom of each metal mop bucket, using a masonry drill.*

2 *With each bucket upright, place crocks in the base, and add the potting mixture, making sure that no air pockets are left around the colanders. Plant up one bucket with one coleus towards the back, two celosias in front of it, and three French marigolds around the edge. You could fill the other bucket with everlastings (RIGHT).*

Coleus *(Coleus blumei)*
An annual grown for its red, purple, lime-green, yellow, and orange variegated leaves.

Celosia *(Celosia cristata)*
Feathery spikes of flowers in bright red, yellow, pink, or apricot appear all summer long.

Everlasting flower *(Helichrysum bracteatum* Monstrosum Series)
The daisy-like flowers come in a wide range of colours.

French marigold
(Tagetes patula 'Spanish Brocade')
The double, orange flowers open for four months.

Informal Bucket Plantings

✄ The orange and red everlasting flowers in one mop bucket, and French marigolds, celosia, and coleus in the other, will put on a colourful display through the summer and into the autumn. These arrangements should not be overwatered. Give the plants a weekly liquid feed.

MAKING A WOODEN WINDOW BOX

I T CAN BE DIFFICULT to find manufactured, wooden window boxes that exactly fit the window sills of your house. One way around this problem is to buy a simple, plastic window box that approximately fits your window-sill, and then make a wooden cover for it. If no plastic box is suitable for your window-sill, construct your own wooden window box to the required measurements. Use an exterior plywood, an oriented strand board (wafer board), or one of the beautiful although more expensive hardwoods, such as cedar or teak.

✄ If you want a natural wood finish, paint the exterior with a wood preservative. Alternatively, apply a primer and an exterior matt or gloss top coat in your chosen colour.

∽ WOODEN FRAME FOR A PLASTIC WINDOW BOX ∽

This simple, wooden frame fits neatly over a manufactured, plastic window box. It is made from oriented strand board (wafer board) to give it a distinctive texture and patterning that will show through paint; for a plain, more even finish and a smoother painting surface, use exterior plywood or a hardwood, instead. Ask a timber merchant to cut the pieces of wood to your specifications. For ideas on how to paint and decorate your finished wooden window box frame, SEE PAGES 164-5.

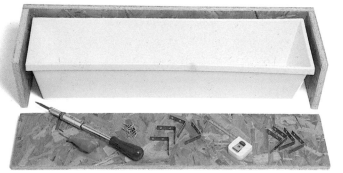

1 For this wooden, window-box frame you will need two sides, one front, and one back. Make the sides 1.2cm (½in) higher and 1.2cm (½in) wider than the inner plastic box. Make the front and back 1.2cm (½in) higher than the inner plastic box, and the sides longer by 1.2cm (½in) plus twice the thickness of the wood.

<table>
<tr><td>

YOU WILL NEED

Tape measure
Four pieces of oriented strand board (wafer board), cut to size
Eight metal brackets
Wood screws
Bradawl
Screwdriver
Paintbrush
Wood preservative, or primer and matt or gloss top coat
</td></tr>
</table>

Dahlia (*Dahlia* 'Redskin') Grown for its deep bronze-green foliage as well as its glorious blooms.

Sage (*Salvia officinalis* 'Tricolor') The variegated leaves are delicious used as a herb.

2 Construct the frame, using two metal brackets in each corner. With a bradawl, mark and puncture the positions of the screws for the metal brackets. The bottom brackets should be 2cm (¾in) above the base; the top brackets should be at least 2.5cm (1in) below the rim.

3 Screw the brackets into position. Secure one of the short sides last of all: with the rest of the box constructed, you will find this is the least tricky part to reach with a screwdriver.

Green Finish
✄ Painted a very dark green, this wooden window box sets off the rich flower colours and variegated foliage in this autumn planting of dahlias, trailing pelargoniums, sage, snapdragons, and sweet alyssum. Place the window box in a sunny position, water frequently in dry weather, and give the plants a weekly feed.

4 The completed frame can be treated with a wood preservative for a natural finish, or painted with a primer and matt or gloss top coat in the colour of your choice.

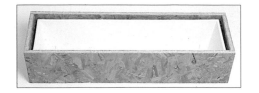

Ivy-leaved pelargonium (*Pelargonium* 'Elégante') A trailing, ivy-leaved variety with delicate, pink flowers.

❧ WOODEN WINDOW BOX ❧

To construct the sides of the window box, follow STEPS 1-3, WOODEN FRAME FOR A PLASTIC WINDOW BOX. Cut one more piece of wood for the base, to fit inside the frame. Exterior plywood gives a smooth paint finish.

YOU WILL NEED

Wood drill	Dark green undercoat
Five pieces of exterior	Dark green matt
plywood, cut to fit the	top coat
window sill	Crocks
Bradawl	Potting mixture of high
Wood screws	nutritional value
Twelve metal brackets	Three dahlias
Screwdriver	Two sages
Tape measure	Two ivy-leaved
Paintbrush	pelargoniums
Bitumen paint	Two snapdragons
Primer	One sweet alyssum

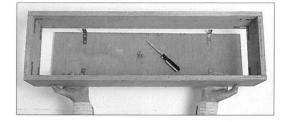

1 *Attach four metal brackets to the base, positioning two on each of the long sides. Fit the frame on to the base of the box, mark the positions of the screw holes with a bradawl, and screw to secure.*

2 *Turn the window box upside down and, using a wood drill, make three 1.2cm (½in) holes in the base for drainage. If the box is less than 60cm (24in) long, only two drainage holes are necessary. Too many holes in the wood will hasten the rotting process.*

3 *Paint the inside of the window box with bitumen paint, and the exterior and all the edges with a primer, and then a dark green matt top coat.*

Snapdragon (*Antirrhinum majus* 'Trumpet Serenade')
Flowers in a range of colours appear for three months.

Sweet alyssum (*Lobularia maritima* 'Wonderland')
The flowers are honey-scented.

DECORATING WOODEN WINDOW BOXES

Most containers made from non-porous materials, such as wood, are easy to paint and decorate. The simplest decoration is a plain surface, painted in a shade that complements the existing colours of the site, or the plants that you are likely to be growing. White, cream, dark green, and black are safe choices as they will relate to most colours.

✗ A more adventurous design would be to paint *trompe l'oeil* panelling or, perhaps, a stencilled decoration on your window box. Beware of including painted flowers in your pattern – they tend to compete for attention with the real ones on the plants.

✗ Always prepare the surface of the container with an exterior wood primer and an exterior top coat. This should remain in good condition for a couple of years, before it needs repainting.

Rustic Effect
✗ Screw on pieces of weathered board to achieve this rustic effect (LEFT). First, glue the strips into place, and then use two screws to attach each board firmly to the inside of the frame.

***Trompe l'Oeil* Panelling**
✗ To create a panelled effect (RIGHT), mark out the panels with a pencil. Mask the edges with tape. Paint two adjacent sides of each panel a lighter shade of the background, and the other two sides a darker shade. This gives a three-dimensional appearance.

Skimmia (*Skimmia reevesiana*)
A self-pollinating variety, producing a good crop of berries in winter.

Cyclamen (*Cyclamen* •
hederifolium var. *album*)
Grown for its attractive,
silver-marbled foliage
and pure white flowers.

Stained Lemon Crate

⚞ A plain wooden crate (ABOVE), used for
packing lemons, makes an effective container
for these white, autumn-flowering cyclamen. I
painted this crate with a wood preservative
and green stain, mixed together.

• **Ornamental cabbage**
(*Brassica oleracea*)
These evergreen biennials provide
warm pinks, pale greens, and
creams for winter planting schemes.

Design for a Winter Window Box

⚞ When the top coat of paint on the window
box is dry, either hand paint it, working out
your pattern on paper first, or decorate it with
a stencil design. Make a stencil by cutting a
pattern out of an oiled, stencil board with a
sharp knife. For foliage, you can trace around
real leaves first, then transfer the design using
carbon paper on to the board.

EVERGREEN TOPIARY

THE ANCIENT ART OF TOPIARY – when plants are encouraged to grow into formal shapes – has been practised since early Roman times. It is not as difficult as it might first appear; indeed, in a sense, it is just pruning taken to the extreme. Clipping a plant into a simple ball or pyramid design is only a question of encouraging growth within the confines of the final shape, and discouraging all other growth. With strong-growing plants, no staking or wiring is necessary. For more complicated topiary – animal shapes, for example – or plants with weaker main stems, some support, such as a stake or wire frame, should be given.

❦ Box, bay, privet, and yew all grow happily in containers and are suitable for training into special shapes. Evergreen climbers like ivy or, in frost-free climates, creeping fig, can also be used to great effect, grown from a pot and trained over a specially shaped, wire frame to make almost any architectural or animal shape.

Clipped Conifers
❦ This decorative front door and porch with an ornate scalloped roof (LEFT) cries out for topiary on each side. Flanking the door are two striking conifers, *Cupressocyparis leylandii* 'Castlewellan', which have each been trained to form two spheres.

Conical Shrub
❦ To train box *(Buxus sempervirens)* into a conical shape (ABOVE), encourage the central main shoot to grow to the required height and clip the side shoots to shape as the plant develops. As the main stem of box is strong, staking is not necessary.

❧ AN IVY CONE ❧

Cover a wire frame with a climber to form a bold architectural shape. Ivy is one of the best climbers to use, as it grows quickly and thickly, and is also evergreen, providing interest throughout the year. The chicken-wire frame constructed for this ivy (BELOW) is made in two sections.

1 *For the bottom section of the frame, cut a 2.4m- (8ft-) length of chicken wire and roll it into a cylinder with a 35cm (14in) diameter. You should end up with a double layer of chicken wire, between which you can sandwich a 1.2cm- (½in-) layer of moss.*

2 *Sandwich the moss firmly between the two layers of chicken wire until you reach the end. Bind the ends of the chicken wire together and the bottom of the cylinder with garden wire to prevent any of the moss from falling out, and make the ring secure.*

3 *Mould the cylinder into shape. Form tucks towards the top so that the cylinder begins to slope inwards. Make a second, smaller cylinder from chicken wire and moss to go on top of the first one. Fold the top to a point and wire on to the bottom cylinder. It is now ready to support the ivy.*

Glossy Green Cone

❦ Ivy (*Hedera helix* 'Deltoidea') will cover the frame in three years. This variety is ideal for a shady or semi-shady site, but it will also grow in sunshine.

4 *Fill the terracotta pot with potting mixture over a bed of crocks. Thread wire through the hole of the metal pole and place it in the centre of the pot. Plant the ivies around the edge.*

5 *Next, place the completed chicken-wire frame in the pot, with its base sitting on the surface of the potting mixture. Use wire to attach the top of the metal rod to the top of the frame.*

YOU WILL NEED
•
3.5m×30cm (12×1ft) chicken wire
Moss
Garden wire
55cm- (22in-) diameter, terracotta pot
Rich potting mixture, and crocks
Metal rod, 107cm (39in) long, with a hole in the top
Five ivies

CONSTRUCTING A HERB TOWER

I ALWAYS LIKE TO HAVE POTS OF HERBS next to the kitchen door, so that I can take one step outside and pick a sprig or two while cooking. Most herbs are sun lovers, so a sunny site is of prime importance to grow a good crop. The smaller species – thyme, chives, oregano, and sage – can be grown in a group in a herb pot or, as here, in a herb tower made from chicken wire and moss. The larger-growing shrubs and trees, such as rosemary and bay, are best given a pot to themselves. Mint, also, should be grown on its own as it can be extremely invasive. Many of the smaller herbs, such as oregano, chives, parsley, and tarragon, even though they are perennials and biennials, produce the best flavour if planted in spring and grown as annuals.

Chives (*Allium schoenoprasum*)
Remove all the flowers to
encourage plentiful foliage.

1 *To make the frame, sandwich moss between two layers of chicken wire. Stitch the base and sides together with garden wire and cut holes for plants in the sides. Line the tower with plastic, and then punch to make drainage holes. Place a layer of crocks in the bottom of the container.*

2 *Fill the chicken-wire and moss frame with potting mixture up to the first side hole. Thread the small and trailing plants through the side holes, building up the soil around them until the tower is filled to within 10-13cm (4-5in) of the top. Plant the larger herbs in the top of the tower.*

3 *Leave a gap of 2cm (¾in) between the top of the potting mixture and the rim of the tower for watering. The herbs should be ready for picking within a few weeks.*

Purple sage
(*Salvia officinalis* 'Purpurascens')
An edible and decorative herb.

Thyme (*Thymus drucei*)
Although a wiry plant,
the leaves have an
excellent flavour.

Marjoram
(Origanum vulgare)
Removing the
flowers will help
keep the plant
bushy.

Decorative Window Sill

A selection of herbs growing in small pots on a sunny window sill can be both decorative and practical. From left to right: purple basil, mint, thyme, tarragon, angelica, and ruby chard.

Thyme *(Thymus vulgaris aureus)*
An intensely aromatic herb.

Variegated mint *(Mentha* x *gentilis* 'Variegata')
This variety has leaves
with a mild flavour.

Parsley *(Petroselinum crispum)*
Planted at the back, out of
sight, a useful biennial, best
picked in its first season.

Cultivation Tips

Water this herb tower frequently, but never allow the potting mixture to become waterlogged, and feed with liquid fertilizer every fortnight. Turn every week to give all the plants the advantage of sun. Do not overpick or the herbs will die.

YOU WILL NEED
•

2.25m×30cm (7½×1ft) chicken wire
Moss
Garden wire
Plastic for lining the tower
Crocks
Potting mixture of medium
nutritional value
One chive plant
One variegated mint
One purple sage
One marjoram
Two thymes
Two parsleys

TRAINING STANDARDS

STANDARD PLANTS ARE NOT AS DIFFICULT to grow as many people assume, although it does help if you have a greenhouse. Standards are more susceptible to frost damage than low-growing plants, and therefore need to be overwintered under glass in colder climates.

You start off standards from cuttings taken in late summer and, at first, concentrate on encouraging the main growing tip. Allow the plant to grow approximately 15cm (6in) tall, then remove any side shoots as they appear. Stake the main stem well and give the plant plenty of water and food (feed twice a week during the growing season), but do not let the potting mixture become soggy. When the leader reaches 15-23cm (6-9in) below the required height of the standard, leave the side shoots to grow and bush out into a mop-head. You may need to make a spherical cage from thick wire to support the side shoots of the mop-head.

• Zonal pelargonium
(Pelargonium 'Deacon Bonanza') In a sunny situation, this produces a profusion of vivid pink flowers.

∽ MOCK TREE FERN ∽

YOU WILL NEED
•
1m- (36in-) long
birch bough
25cm (10in) pot
Plaster of
Paris mix
Plant-pot saucer
Screws
Pot-fixing clips
40cm (16in) pot
Medium-rich
potting mixture
Ivy
Boston fern

Make an imitation tree fern, by placing a Boston fern at the end of a birch bough. Boston ferns can only be kept outside in summer and autumn. If you want a plant that can stay outside all year, use ivy instead. Wandering Jew would also look effective displayed in this way, but it, too, is only semi-hardy.

1 *Fix a 1m- (36in-) long tree bough in a pot filled with a plaster of Paris mix. Screw a saucer with pot-fixing clips to the bough. Place the plaster-filled pot in the larger pot.*

2 *Fill the large pot with potting mixture and plant ivy around the edge. Secure a Boston fern on to the saucer. Place in a sheltered, shady or semi-shady position, out of strong winds. Water the plants well, and occasionally clip the ivy to keep it neat and tidy.*

Flowering Mop-heads

Pelargoniums and fuchsias make particularly good mop-heads, as they both flower profusely all summer long. The pelargoniums should be kept in sun, but the fuchsias and hydrangeas prefer semi-shade. Although hydrangeas are hardy, it is best to protect standards from frost, keeping them in a greenhouse over winter.

Fuchsia (*Fuchsia* 'Citation')
A strong-growing variety that is suitable for training into an attractive mop-head.

Ivy (*Hedera helix* 'Gracilis')
Planted in two of these tubs to cover the potting mixture.

Hydrangea (*Hydrangea macrophylla* 'Hamburg')
Keep in good, dappled light and water plentifully. This specimen is only two years old.

Ivy (*Hedera helix* 'Deltoidea')
A variety distinguished by its heart-shaped, green leaves.

SUPPORTING PLANTS IN POTS

C LIMBERS, TALL ANNUALS and perennials, and young shrubs and trees with supple stems, all require support when grown in containers. As the extent of the support's base will be limited by the size of the container, traditional means used for plants growing in borders are not always possible, so you have to be a little more imaginative and inventive.

⚵ The simplest form of support is a single stake or cane, driven into the potting mixture down to the base of the pot – the main stem of the plant is tied to the stake. This method is good for plants that eventually support themselves, such as young trees. For a stronger, more permanent structure, make a pyramid- or fan-shaped trellis. Ensure that the stakes are long enough to reach from the bottom of the pot to above the top of the plant.

Silver Tree

⚵ Helichrysum *(Helichrysum petiolare)* is a half-hardy shrub that can reach 1.5m (5ft) in just one summer season, if trained up a pyramid of four bamboo canes. Tie the main shoot to the central stake and stop side shoots at 13cm (5in) long, until the plant reaches the required height. Thereafter, clip or leave it to spread informally. Stop any flowers. Grow in a sunny site, feed and water regularly, and protect from frost in winter.

∽ MAKING A TRELLIS ∽

1 *Lay out four canes and fan them so that the bottom ends fit in your container. Lay the sticks, cut in increasing lengths, across the main canes at regular intervals. Mark the positions where they cross the canes.*

2 *Attach the bottom lateral stick to each of the canes with wire. Make a loop around the back of the cane, crossing the ends over the lateral stick and bringing them down behind.*

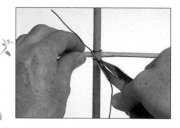

3 *Twist the wire tightly behind the cane on the reverse side. First, attach the base lateral stick and then the top one, to form a rigid frame, before securing the rest of the canes in position.*

Fragrant Climber

❀ The semi-evergreen Japanese honeysuckle (*Lonicera japonica* 'Halliana') produces strongly scented flowers throughout the summer and autumn; an excellent climber for a pot.

PLANT CARE

❧

FROM SEED OR CUTTING TO MATURE SPECIMEN, your summer annuals, spring bulbs, perennials, shrubs and trees must be looked after properly if they are to give you their best, over the longest possible period. Pruning, propagation, watering, feeding, planting, and pest and disease control are neither difficult nor complicated. Follow the few simple measures outlined here, and your plants should be both healthy and happy.

ESSENTIAL GARDEN TOOLS
A watering can, trowel, secateurs, garden string, and stakes are necessities for the day to day care of plants in containers.

PESTS AND DISEASES

PLANTS IN CONTAINERS are as susceptible to most pests and diseases as those growing in the open ground. However, slugs and snails, which crawl along the ground, may not present such a problem.

✠ A few simple measures can help to deter both pests and diseases. Start out with a container, crocks, and soil that are as clean as possible. Scrub the pot and drainage crocks in a solution of water and disinfectant to eradicate any fungal spores. And always use a potting mixture that has been sterilized – most bagged mixes are safe – so that no diseases are carried in the soil. Remember that re-used potting mixtures can be troublesome. Petunias, in particular, should never be planted in soil that previously has been used for petunias or they can get petunia wilt.

✠ Whenever possible, try to use organic methods to control pests in the garden. Soapy household water or any natural soap spray is useful for killing aphids, and slugs and snails are attracted by grapefruit. Make a trap by cutting the fruit in half, scooping out the flesh and placing the peel, like a small igloo, on the ground. Each morning, remove all slugs or snails in the trap. A flowerpot stuffed with newspaper, and placed upside down on a stick will attract earwigs, and draw them away from dahlias. If you raise your containers just slightly off the ground, this should also deter earwigs from gathering under the pots. Keep the area around your pots free of dead leaves and debris, which might provide shelter and warm, moist, living conditions for unwanted wildlife.

Leaf Miner
✠ The larvae of various species of moths and flies burrow into the fabric of leaves, marking them with a patch or a fine network of lines. The plants most likely to be affected by leaf miners are columbines, lilacs, laburnum, and chrysanthemums. Infestations do not always cause much damage. Treat with a chemical spray if the damage becomes substantial.

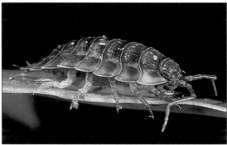

Woodlouse
✠ Hard-coated pests, woodlice live in damp, shady places and feed off organic debris. Large colonies of them may congregate in the moist crannies under containers and enter pots through the drainage holes. They are night feeders and will eat most parts of plants, including the roots, stems, and leaves. Dusts and sprays are available to control them.

Earwig
✠ These insects are not a major pest of plants growing in containers, although they will eat dahlia and chrysanthemum flowers and leaves at night. Place an inverted flower pot, filled with straw, on a stake near the plant. The earwigs will congregate in the pot overnight. Remove the pot in the morning.

Slug
✠ Smaller slugs do the most damage. They emerge from damp, shady places among dead leaves or any rotting vegetation at night, to eat the young stems, leaves, and buds, and also roots, bulbs, and corms below the soil. To keep slugs in check, ensure plants are clean and free of dead leaves, and look beneath and behind pots for them.

Aphid

Several different species of aphid are troublesome on garden plants. Commonly called greenfly and blackfly, these extremely invasive insects suck the sap of young growth and the sap around flower buds, disfiguring the plant and sometimes causing the buds to rot. They also excrete a sticky honeydew that encourages sooty moulds to grow and can transmit virus diseases. They thrive in warm weather, and annuals, perennials, and shrubs are all suscepible. Keep a regular check for them and treat as soon as you see them. There are several organic products made from natural soaps that kill aphids, as well as a mass of chemical insecticides.

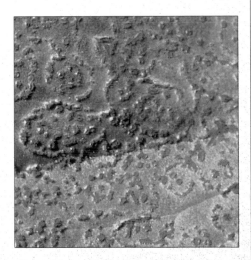

Scale Insect

These insects may infest bay trees, camellias, and other evergreens, leaving a sticky, black deposit on the foliage. The female insects are protected by a tough, scale covering that adheres strongly to the leaf. Kill scale insects with an insecticide when they are hatching during the summer, or remove the scales by hand.

Whitefly

Related to aphids but looking more like miniature moths, whitefly live on the undersides of leaves and feed on plant sap. They excrete a sticky honeydew, which adheres to leaf stems and flowers and can attract sooty mould. They breed quickly in summer, but infestations can occur from late spring. Control them with the same insecticides that kill aphids.

Mildew

Flourishing on roses, begonias, and chrysanthemums, powdery and downy mildews are caused by various fungi. Contrary to what many people believe, mildews are most prevalent in dry weather. Spray plants and any fallen leaves from early spring onwards.

Rust

A fungal infection that causes spots and marking on leaves. Begin anti-fungal spraying in early spring. Burn all leaves that are infected, and destroy the entire plant if it is badly infected and the rust appears two years running. Snapdragons, sweet William, mahonia, and roses are most likely to be affected.

PLANTING AND REPOTTING

GIVE YOUR PLANTS the very best possible start by planting them properly. Ensure that the container is completely clean and that the inside is free of old soil, which might harbour disease. Porous-surfaced containers, such as stone and terracotta, should be cleaned especially well. Scrub the container with a mild disinfectant. If you would like the outside of an old terracotta pot to keep its weathered appearance, just clean the inside.

PLANTING UP CONTAINERS

It is a good idea to give porous-surfaced containers a good soak before planting them up. When they are dry, containers quickly take a great deal of moisture out of the potting mixture.

✗ Next, place a layer of drainage material in the bottom of the container. Pieces of broken terracotta make one of the best drainage mediums, but pebbles or even pieces of polystyrene can be used. Container plants grow best when planted in a peat-based or soil-based potting mixture. The soil-based mixtures are usually neutral, although some are made up with either a higher acid or alkaline content. The peat-based mixtures tend towards acidity.

✗ Both the peat-based and the soil-based potting mixtures are sold in varying degrees of nutritional value. The one with the lowest nutritional value is ideal for raising seeds and potting on seedlings. Potting mixtures of medium nutritional value are best for young plants, and the high nutrition potting mixtures are used mostly for mature plants.

✗ Soil-based potting mixtures tend to be heavy and can easily become compacted and solid, making efficient watering difficult. The peat-based ones, however, dry out very quickly, and once dry are not easy to make moist again. I find that an equal mixture of the two makes one of the best mediums unless the plant has particular requirements.

REPOTTING

When plants become root-bound and their roots start growing out of the bottom of the drainage holes, it is time to transfer them to a larger container. Most plants will be happy if they are planted into a pot that is larger than the previous one. For visual reasons, it is best not to use a pot that is too big or it will look unbalanced.

❧ REPOTTING LARGE PLANTS ❧

If a large plant has become completely pot-bound, so that it is attached to the pot and is too heavy to turn upside down and tap to remove the root ball, use the method outlined below to remove it.

1 *This large cordyline needs repotting. Its roots have started growing out of the drainage holes of the pot. Plants also need repotting when the roots start growing in a spiral around the inner edge of the pot.*

3 *If the tapping method fails, cut the pot away from the root ball. With sharp secateurs, cut a straight line down the side of the pot. If necessary, cut another line down the opposite side of the pot.*

2 *Tie back the foliage with string or with one of the leaves. To release the plant, hold it by the stem, just above the potting mixture, lift and tap round the edge of the pot. It is easier if someone helps you.*

~ CLEANING CONTAINERS ~

*⚘ Clean all previously
used containers
thoroughly before you
plant them up. Scrub
the inside, and the
outside if desired, with
a weak solution of
disinfectant to remove
any disease or pests that might be on the
container's surface. Rinse with clean
water after scrubbing. Thoroughly clean
the drainage crocks as well. Bear in
mind that larger pieces of terracotta are
easier to scrub than smaller pieces.*

~ REPOTTING SMALL PLANTS ~

Water the plant thoroughly beforehand to make sure that it is in a healthy state.
Never repot when the temperature is below freezing as many plants are
susceptible to frost. Transfer the plant to a container that is at least one size
larger than the one it was growing in, and make sure that the soil comes up to
the same level on the plant as it did in the previous pot.

*1 Firm potting mixture on to a bed of
clean crocks in the new container
so that when positioned, the old soil
mark on the plant comes to just below
the top edge of the pot.*

*2 Water the plant well by soaking it
in a bucket of water until bubbles
stop forming. Place your fingers firmly
across the base of the stem, and then
turn the pot upside down.*

*3 Tap the pot on a firm edge, such as
the top of the bucket, to free the ball
of soil from the pot. If this does not
work, try pushing a small stick up
through one of the drainage holes.*

*4 Gently loosen the roots at the base
and at the sides with your fingers.
This will encourage the roots to grow
outwards and downwards once
planted, instead of in a spiral.*

*5 Place the plant on the firmed soil
in the new pot, making sure that it
stands straight, and carefully fill in
the sides with potting mixture to just
below the top of the pot. Firm.*

WATERING

PLANTS IN CONTAINERS require more careful watering than those grown in open ground, as the soil in pots is more likely to dry out or become waterlogged. On the positive side, however, it is easier to control the amount of water and liquid feed you give to container-grown plants.

THE CORRECT BALANCE

For the majority of plant species and varieties, the soil in a container needs to be kept just moist, but never soggy, during their growing and flowering seasons (spring and summer). As plants hate to have their roots sitting in water, avoid placing a saucer under the pot, which traps excess water.

The leaves often cover much of the top surface of the potting mixture, so the plants in containers do not receive as much natural rainwater as plants in beds. Check for adequate moisture, therefore, even in wet weather. For plants that need feeding in the growing and flowering seasons, add a measure of liquid or soluble solid food to their water. Different plants have different requirements, but the most usual is a weekly feed. For specific requirements, SEE PRACTICAL MATTERS with each planting scheme.

✠ In winter, when the temperature is above freezing, give the plants a little water, perhaps once a fortnight. However, never water in freezing weather.

Bucket of Water
✠ *Gently submerge the pot in a bucket, two-thirds full of water. The water should come over the top of the container. When no more bubbles appear, the root ball is soaked. Drain the plant.*

Hanging Baskets
✠ *Use a compression unit to water hanging baskets that are out of reach. This method squirts water from a bottle, up a tube, which has a curved end, making it possible to direct water straight into the potting mixture. Hanging baskets dry out much more quickly than other containers because the surface is so porous – make sure that they receive sufficient liquid sustenance. In hot weather, they may need to be watered twice a day.*

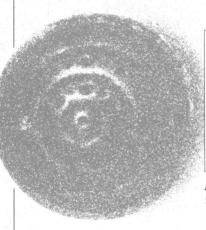

Drip Method
✠ *A commercial drip system is useful for watering plants when you go away. Capillary tubing carries water from a bucket to the potting mixture and the plants. Keep the plants in a shady place.*

Wick System
✠ *Push one end of a paraffin lamp wick into the soil surrounding the plant and trail the other end in a bucket of water. Ensure that the wick is wet and reaches the bottom of the bucket for best results.*

Packed in Peat
✠ *Plants can be kept moist by surrounding them in damp peat. Make sure that they stand on, and are surrounded by, peat. In a shady site, the plants should remain in good condition for several days.*

PRUNING AND DEADHEADING

To encourage plants to grow into an attractive shape and to produce as many flowers as possible, some pruning and deadheading are required. Pruning is generally a matter of common sense: taking away dead, weak, and unsightly growths, and cutting the shrub to maintain a good visual shape. This ensures that strong, healthy growth, carrying the most flowers, can develop unhindered. Some plants, such as hydrangeas and camellias, produce flowers on the previous year's growth, while others, such as rhododendrons and some of the roses, for example, flower on the new growth. This determines the time of year when you need to prune them.

❦ Plants with long flowering seasons, such as annuals, have many more flowers if they do not spend their energy on producing seeds. Unless the seedheads are decorative, therefore, remove all the dead flowers to encourage a continuous display through the flowering period.

❧ DEADHEADING ANNUALS ❧

Remove dead flowers as they appear, to prolong the flowering season. Always use sharp cutting implements, such as secateurs and scissors, so that scarring is kept to a minimum. This can be tedious but it certainly pays dividends.

❦ *Pelargoniums should be constantly deadheaded if they are to produce a display of flowers over several months. Just snap off the flower stalk at the joint.*

❦ *Like these pansies, most annuals can be deadheaded with scissors. Snip off dying and dead flowers to the flower stem joint. This prevents the seedheads from forming.*

❧ PRUNING EVERGREEN SHRUBS ❧

Like the Mexican orange blossom *(Choisya ternata)* below, most evergreen shrubs require only a little pruning. After the new spring growth has hardened, prune with secateurs to improve the shape and remove dead wood.

1 *Encourage Mexican orange blossom to form a well-rounded head by removing crossing growths, and take back longer stems to just above a leaf joint.*

2 *Take out spindly and dead wood. The trimmed shrub still may look slightly mis-shapen but will soon grow into a bushy form. Prune after flowering.*

❧ PRUNING ROSES IN CONTAINERS ❧

The best roses to grow in containers are low-growing, bush, hybrid tea varieties the cluster-flowered, bush, floribunda varieties, and miniatures. These all need pruning in spring as the new flowering growths start to develop.

1 *Cut out all of the dead and spindly wood from the rose bush and any of its branches that are crossing and rubbing against one another.*

2 *Leaving three or four buds on each stem of the bush, make a clean cut at a slight angle, immediately above a healthy-looking, outward-facing bud.*

3 *The pruned rose bush should form an open fan of branches to allow the new shoots to develop healthily, and produce a good crop of flowers for the next season.*

PROPAGATION

GROWING YOUR OWN PLANTS from scratch is extremely satisfying. There are two basic methods of producing plants. The first, sexual propagation, involves growing plants from seed, a process that can be carried out in the home without too much difficulty. Plants, such as annuals and vegetables, are particularly easy to raise in this way and most will produce flowers and fruit in the first year. If you use seed you have collected yourself, it does not always come true. If you want to be absolutely sure of getting a particular plant variety, buy the seed from a reputable seed merchant.

The second method is vegetative propagation, which involves taking cuttings, layering, or dividing. This method always produces plants that are identical to the host plants. Some species are extremely easy to propagate vegetatively. They include busy Lizzies, wandering Jew, and coleus, cuttings of which root simply in water. Others, such as camellias, are much more difficult and respond better to leaf propagation. Some simple propagation techniques are shown below, but propagation is a large subject, and if you need to know about particular plants, it is best to read a book that covers the subject in more detail.

∽ DIVIDING PERENNIALS ∽

Most perennials benefit from being divided every two or three years. As their root systems expand, the centres die out, leaving healthy growth only around the edges. By dividing the roots, you can remove the dead centres, as well as increasing your stock.

1 *Hardy perennials, such as hostas, can be easily propagated by division in spring. Turn the pot upside down to release the root ball. You may need to tap it out with a stick through the drainage hole if it will not come out easily.*

2 *Gently scrape away any excess potting mixture that clings around the clump of roots, taking care not to damage the main root system. Most perennials are generally pretty tough and it is difficult to do much harm when dividing them.*

3 *Where the roots seem to divide naturally, dig down with a small, sharp spade to part the clump in two. If required, you can divide it further. Plant up again immediately.*

∽ RAISING ANNUALS FROM SEED ∽

To germinate seed, all you need is a seed tray, seed potting mixture, shaded light, and a steady temperature of 18°C (64°F). Cover the seed tray with thin plastic to create humid conditions.

1 *Make shallow drills in a tray of seed potting mixture. Thinly sprinkle in seeds and cover lightly. Water and seal with thin plastic.*

2 *When the first leaf pair opens, prick the seeds out with a forked emery board. Holding by the leaves, place them 4cm (1¹/₂in) apart, in pots of seed potting mixture.*

✎ TAKING CUTTINGS ✎

Tender perennials, such as pelargoniums, can be rooted from softwood cuttings. Semi-ripe cuttings are mostly taken from shrubs and climbers, and rooted in mid to late summer. Hardwood cuttings are taken as leafless, mature shoots from shrubs and trees in autumn and winter.

1 *To take a hardwood or semi-ripe cutting, remove a firm 15-20cm (6-8in) shoot from a shrub, such as senecio. Using a sharp pruning knife, recut the end of the cutting just below a leaf node.*

2 *Gently remove the lower leaves (and the tip if it is a semi-ripe cutting) with a sharp knife, and dip the freshly cut end in hormone rooting powder, coating about 2cm (1in) of the stem.*

3 *Insert in a pot of very well-drained, medium-rich potting mixture with sand and peat. Firm well in position and, ideally, place in a cold frame. The cuttings will take up to one year to root.*

✎ TAKING A LEAF BUD CUTTING ✎

Taking leaf bud cuttings is a good method of propagating camellias, magnolias, and rhododendrons. It is best to take the cuttings in summer when the plants are in full growth.

1 *Cut a leaf with a leaf bud and a heel of the plant's woody stem from a section that has just been removed from the parent. Make sure that you use a sharp pruning knife to achieve a clean cut.*

2 *Dip the heel and some of the leaf base in hormone rooting powder. Insert in a prepared half sand, half peat mix. Keep moist at 18°C (64°F) until the cutting has rooted. It can take several months.*

Cuttings in Water

✎ *You can propagate some plants by placing a stem, cut just below a leaf node with the lower leaves removed, in a glass of water. Rooting is quite rapid in a light, but not sunny, position in summer. Begonias, busy Lizzies, coleus and wandering Jew all respond well.*

PLANT LISTS

❋ *Abutilon* (ABUTILON)
• Hardy to half-hardy, evergreen, semi-evergreen, or deciduous shrubs, perennials, and annuals
• Summer flowers
• Rich, well-drained potting mixture
• Sunny or semi-shady site
• Very floriferous container plant

❋ *Acer* (MAPLE)
• Hardy, deciduous shrubs or trees
• Attractive foliage
• Rich, well-drained potting mixture
• Sunny or semi-shady site
• The fine-leaved varieties do not like too much sun

❋ *Adiantum* (MAIDENHAIR FERN)
• Hardy to half-hardy, deciduous, semi-evergreen, and evergreen ferns
• Attractive foliage
• Moist, neutral to acid potting mixture
• Semi-shady site
• Remove fading fronds

❋ *Agapanthus* (AFRICAN LILY)
• Hardy to half-hardy, clump-forming, evergreen perennials
• Clusters of blue or white, summer flowers
• Moist but well-drained potting mixture
• Sunny site
• Divide in spring

❋ *Agave* (AGAVE)
• Half-hardy to tender, perennial succulents
• Sword-shaped, sharp-toothed leaves
• Well-drained potting mixture
• Sunny site
• Keep frost-free over winter

❋ *Ageratum* (FLOSS FLOWER)
• Half-hardy, bushy annuals
• Clusters of feathery, summer flowers
• Rich, well-drained potting mixture
• Sunny or semi-shady site
• Efficient deadheading ensures continuous flowering

❋ *Aloe* (ALOE)
• Half-hardy to tender, evergreen, rosetted shrubs and perennials
• Succulent foliage and bell-shaped, winter or spring flowers
• Very well-drained potting mixture
• Sunny site
• Highly architectural plants

❋ *Anenome blanda* (WINDFLOWER)
• Hardy perennials grown from tubers
• Cup-shaped, spring flowers
• Well-drained potting mixture with leafmould
• Sunny or semi-shady site
• The fragile flowers are white, blue, and pink

❋ *Anthemis* (CHAMOMILE)
• Hardy perennials, some of which are evergreen
• Summer flowers and fern-like foliage
• Well-drained potting mixture
• Sunny site
• The tangy-scented flowers are wonderful in pot pourri

❋ *Antirrhinum* (SNAPDRAGON)
• Hardy to half-hardy perennials usually grown as annuals
• Spikes of spring to autumn flowers
• Rich, well-drained potting mixture
• Sunny site
• Deadhead to prolong flowering

❋ *Aquilegia* (COLUMBINE)
• Hardy, short-lived perennials
• Spurred, spring and summer flowers
• Well-drained potting mixture
• Sunny or semi-shady site
• Prone to aphid attack

❋ *Artemisia* (SOUTHERNWOOD)
• Hardy perennials and sub-shrubs that are evergreen or semi-evergreen
• Aromatic leaves
• Well-drained potting mixture
• Open, sunny site
• Trim back in spring

❋ *Asparagus* (ASPARAGUS)
• Half-hardy to tender, evergreen perennials
• Fern-like foliage
• Rich, well-drained potting mixture
• Semi-shady site
• Avoid placing in direct sun

❋ *Aspidistra* (ASPIDISTRA)
• Half-hardy evergreen perennials
• Glossy foliage
• Well-drained, acid potting mixture with leafmould
• Semi-shady or deeply shady site
• Water frequently during the growing season

❋ *Aster* (MICHAELMAS DAISY)
• Hardy perennials
• Daisy-like, autumn flowers
• Rich, well-drained potting mixture
• Sunny or semi-shady site
• The low-growing cultivars are the best for containers

❋ *Astilbe* (ASTILBE)
• Hardy perennials
• Plumes of feathery, summer flowers
• Rich, moist potting mixture
• Semi-shady site
• Repot infrequently as they resent disturbance

❋ *Begonia* (BEGONIA)
• Half-hardy to tender, evergreen perennials and annuals
• Summer flowers and attractive foliage
• Rich, well-drained, preferably acid, potting mixture
• Semi-shady or shady site
• Most of them can be overwintered in a frost-free situation

❋ *Bellis perennis* (DOUBLE DAISY)
• Hardy perennials grown as biennials
• Daisy-like, spring flowers
• Rich, well-drained potting mixture
• Sunny or semi-shady site
• Deadhead regularly for continuous blooms

❋ *Bergenia* (BERGENIA)
• Hardy evergreen perennials
• Leathery leaves and purple-pink, winter to spring flowers
• Poor, well-drained potting mixture
• Sunny or shady site
• Divide crowded clumps in spring

❋ *Brassica oleracea* (ORNAMENTAL CABBAGE)
• Hardy annuals, evergreen biennials, or perennials
• Ornamental autumn and winter foliage
• Well-drained, preferably acid potting mixture
• Sunny site
• Raise from seed sown outdoors in spring

❋ *Buxus* (BOX)
• Hardy, evergreen shrubs or trees
• Tiny foliage and neat habit
• Well-drained potting mixture
• Sunny, semi-shady, or shady site
• Excellent for clipping into architectural shapes

❋ *Calceolaria* (CALCEOLARIA)
• Hardy to tender annuals
• Summer flowers
• Well-drained, moisture-retentive potting mixture
• Sunny or shady site
• The extraordinary flowers appear over a long period

❋ *Calendula* (MARIGOLD)
• Hardy, bushy annuals
• Orange, cream, and yellow, spring to autumn flowers
• Any well-drained potting mixture
• Sunny site
• Deadhead to prolong flowering

❋ *Calluna* (HEATHER)
• Hardy, evergreen shrubs
• Bell- to urn-shaped, single or double, summer to autumn flowers
• Rich, well-drained, acid potting mixture
• Open, sunny site
• Enormous number of varieties available

❋ *Camellia* (CAMELLIA)
• Hardy to half-hardy, evergreen shrubs and trees
• Spring flowers and glossy, green foliage
• Well-drained, neutral to acid potting mixture
• Sheltered, semi-shady site
• Propagate by leaf cuttings

❋ *Campanula* (BELLFLOWER)
• Hardy annuals, biennials, and perennials, some of which are evergreen
• Bell- and star-shaped, summer flowers
• Moist but well-drained potting mixture
• Sunny or shady site
• The trailing varieties flower for months

❋ *Celosia* (CELOSIA)
• Half-hardy, erect perennials grown as annuals
• Plumes of summer flowers
• Well-drained potting mixture
• Sheltered, sunny site
• Flowers are red, orange, pink, and salmon

❋ *Ceratostigma* (CERATOSTIGMA)
• Hardy to half-hardy, deciduous, semi-evergreen, and evergreen shrubs
• Blue, late summer and autumn flowers, and autumn foliage
• Well-drained potting mixture
• Sunny site
• Cut out dead wood in the spring

❋ *Chamaecyparis lawsoniana* (LAWSON CYPRESS)
• Hardy conifers with scale- or needle-like foliage
• Year-round foliage
• Well-drained potting mixture
• Sunny site
• Dwarf and low-growing varieties are best for containers

❋ *Cheiranthus cheiri* (WALLFLOWER)
• Hardy perennials or sub-shrubs, some evergreen or semi-evergreen
• Fragrant, spring flowers
• Well-drained potting mixture
• Sunny or semi-shady site
• Plants may get weedy, but the scent is one of the best

❋ *Chlorophytum* (SPIDER PLANT)
• Half-hardy and tender, evergreen perennials
• Glossy foliage
• Rich, well-drained potting mixture
• Any site
• Keep out of direct sun

❋ *Choisya ternata* (MEXICAN ORANGE BLOSSOM)
• Hardy, evergreen shrubs
• Fragrant, spring flowers and shiny foliage
• Well-drained potting mixture
• Sunny site
• Propagate by semi-ripe cuttings in late summer

❋ *Chrysanthemum* (CHRYSANTHEMUM)
• Hardy annuals and perennials, some evergreen
• Summer to autumn flowers
• Well-drained potting mixture
• Sunny site
• All forms do well in pots

❋ *Coleus blumei* (COLEUS)
• Tender perennials, annuals, or evergreen sub-shrubs
• Colourful foliage
• Well-drained potting mixture
• Sunny or semi-shady site
• Remove flowers to promote bushiness and leaf colour

❋ *Convallaria* (LILY-OF-THE-VALLEY)
• Hardy perennials grown from rhizomes
• Fragrant, spring flowers
• Moist potting mixture with leafmould
• Sunny or semi-shady site
• The best-scented plant of all

✿ **Cordyline** (CORDYLINE)
• Hardy to half-hardy, evergreen shrubs and trees
• Strap-shaped foliage
• Rich, well-drained potting mixture
• Sunny or semi-shady site
• Hardier than supposed

✿ **Cotoneaster** (COTONEASTER)
• Hardy, deciduous or evergreen shrubs
• Autumn fruits and attractive foliage
• Well-drained potting mixture
• Sunny or semi-shady site
• Useful for year-round interest in exposed sites

✿ **Crocus** (CROCUS)
• Hardy perennials grown from corms
• Spring and autumn flowers
• Well-drained potting mixture
• Sunny site
• Grows well in low bowls

✿ **Cuphea ignea** (CIGAR FLOWER)
• Half-hardy to tender, evergreen, bushy sub-shrubs
• Tubular, orange-red, summer flowers
• Rich, well-drained potting mixture
• Sunny site
• Water freely during the growing season

✿ **Cupressus** (CYPRESS)
• Hardy, evergreen shrubs and trees
• Attractive foliage and interesting form
• Any potting mixture
• Sunny site
• All have fragrant leaves

✿ **Cyclamen** (CYCLAMEN)
• Hardy to tender perennials grown from corms
• Autumn flowers
• Well-drained potting mixture with leafmould
• Sunny or semi-shady site
• Keep the corms dry after flowers and leaves die down

✿ **Cytisus** (BROOM)
• Hardy, deciduous or evergreen shrubs
• Abundant pea-like, spring flowers
• Poor, well-drained potting mixture
• Sunny site
• Transplant with care as they dislike disturbance

✿ **Dahlia** (DAHLIA)
• Half-hardy, bushy perennials grown from tubers
• Summer and autumn flowerheads
• Well-drained potting mixture
• Sunny site
• Store tubers in dry, frost-free place over winter

✿ **Dianthus** (PINK)
• Hardy, evergreen, clump-forming perennnials
• Summer flowers and attractive foliage
• Well-drained potting mixture
• Sunny site
• Choose scented varieties and deadhead

✿ **Diascia** (DIASCIA)
• Hardy to half-hardy annuals and perennials, some evergreen
• Tubular, summer flowers
• Well-drained potting mixture
• Sunny site
• Produce huge quantities of flowers over a long period

✿ **Dryopteris** (MALE FERN)
• Hardy, deciduous or semi-evergreen ferns
• Shuttlecock-like crowns
• Moist potting mixture
• Semi-shady or shady site
• Remove fading fronds

✿ **Echeveria** (ECHEVERIA)
• Tender, rosetted, perennial succulents
• Attractive foliage and summer flowers
• Very well-drained potting mixture
• Sunny site
• These succulents are well equipped to survive drought

✿ **Elaeagnus** (ELAEAGNUS)
• Hardy, deciduous or evergreen shrubs and trees
• Attractive foliage, fruits, and fragrant, spring to autumn flowers
• Rich, well-drained potting mixture
• Evergreens in sun or shade, deciduous species in sun
• Evergreen varieties can be made into topiary specimens

✿ **Erica** (HEATHER)
• Hardy to half-hardy, evergreen, woody-stemmed shrubs
• Flowers and year-round foliage
• Poor, well-drained, acid potting mixture
• Sunny site
• Varieties flower in every month of the year

✿ **Erythronium** (DOG'S TOOTH VIOLET)
• Hardy perennials grown from tubers
• Pendent flowers and sometimes mottled leaves
• Well-drained potting mixture with leafmould
• Semi-shady site
• Do not allow tubers to get too hot in summer

✿ **Euonymus** (EUONYMUS)
• Hardy, evergreen or deciduous shrubs or trees
• Foliage

• Well-drained potting mixture
• Sunny or semi-shady site
• The evergreen varieties are best for containers

✿ **Euphorbia** (SPURGE)
• Hardy shrubs, succulents, and perennials, some semi-evergreen or evergreen, and annuals
• Foliage and spring flowers
• Moist but well-drained potting mixture
• Sunny or semi-shady site
• Milky sap can irritate skin

✿ **Eustoma** (EUSTOMA)
• Tender annuals and perennials
• Poppy-like, summer flowers
• Well-drained potting mixture
• Sunny site
• Purple, pink, and white flowers offset by silver foliage

✿ **Fatsia** (FATSIA)
• Hardy, evergreen shrubs
• Bold foliage
• Rich, well-drained potting mixture
• Sunny or shady site
• Propagate by semi-ripe cuttings in summer

✿ **Ficus pumila** (CREEPING FIG)
• Tender, evergreen climbers
• Vibrant foliage
• Rich potting mixture
• Semi-shady site
• A plant that likes growing in soggy potting mixture

✿ **Fritillaria imperialis** (CROWN IMPERIAL)
• Hardy perennials grown from bulbs
• Pendent, mainly bell-shaped, spring flowers
• Well-drained potting mixture
• Sunny or semi-shady site
• Potting mixture must not get too dry in winter and spring

✿ **Fritillaria meleagris** (SNAKE'S HEAD FRITILLARY)
• Hardy perennials grown from bulbs
• Pendent, bell-shaped, spring flowers
• Moisture retentive, well-drained potting mixture
• Sunny or semi-shady site
• Allow to dry after flowering has finished

✿ **Fuchsia** (FUCHSIA)
• Hardy to half-hardy, deciduous or evergreen shrubs, sometimes grown as annuals
• Summer and autumn flowers
• Moist but well-drained potting mixture
• Sheltered, semi-shady or shady site

• Keep half-hardy specimens out of frost in winter and cut back in late spring

✿ **Gaultheria** (GAULTHERIA)
• Hardy, evergreen shrubs
• Attractive foliage, spring to summer flowers, and fruits
• Moist, acid potting mixture
• Semi-shady or shady site
• Keep potting mixture damp, especially in summer

✿ **Gazania** (GAZANIA)
• Half-hardy perennials, often grown as annuals
• Daisy-like summer flowers
• Sandy potting mixture
• Sunny site
• Flowers open only in sun

✿ **Geranium** (CRANESBILL)
• Half-hardy to tender perennials, some semi-evergreen
• Spring and summer flowers
• Any well-drained potting mixture
• Sunny site; some species do better in shade
• Many have beautiful leaves and flowers for long periods

✿ **Gleditsia** (LOCUST)
• Hardy, deciduous trees
• Attractive foliage
• Rich, well-drained potting mixture
• Sunny site
• Spectacular autumn colour

✿ **Gypsophila** (GYPSOPHILA)
• Hardy annuals or perennials
• Delicate spring and summer flowers and foliage
• Well drained potting mixture
• Sunny site
• The species that are rock plants do well in pots

✿ **X Halimiocistus** (HALIMIOCISTUS)
• Hardy, hybrid genus of evergreen shrubs
• Saucer-shaped, summer flowers
• Well-drained potting mixture
• Sheltered, sunny site
• Plants are smothered in flowers for many weeks

✿ **Hebe** (HEBE)
• Hardy to half-hardy, evergreen shrubs
• Neat foliage and often dense spikes, panicles, or racemes of flowers
• Well-drained potting mixture
• Sunny site
• Protect from cold in winter

✿ **Hedera** (IVY)
• Hardy, evergreen, woody-stemmed, trailing perennials or self-clinging climbers
• Lush foliage and habit
• Well-drained, alkaline potting mixture

• Any site is suitable
• A useful evergreen trailer to plant at the front of containers

✿ **Helichrysum** (HELICHRYSUM)
• Hardy to tender annuals, perennials, or evergreen sub-shrubs and shrubs
• Summer and autumn flowers and silvery foliage
• Well-drained potting mixture
• Sunny site
• Needs plenty of sun

✿ **Heliotropium** (HELIOTROPE)
• Hardy to tender annuals
• Fragrant, summer flowers
• Rich, well-drained potting mixture
• Sunny site
• Grow for its perfume

✿ **Helleborus** (HELLEBORE)
• Hardy perennials, some of which are evergreen
• Winter and spring flowers
• Well-drained, moisture-retentive potting mixture
• Semi-shady site
• Exceedingly beautiful flowers and decorative foliage

✿ **Heuchera** (HEUCHERA)
• Hardy, evergreen perennials
• Attractive foliage and red, pink, and white flowers
• Moist but well-drained potting mixture
• Sunny or semi-shady site
• Bronze or purple foliage

✿ **Hosta** (HOSTA)
• Hardy perennials
• Decorative foliage and spires of summer flowers
• Moist but well-drained potting mixture
• Semi-shady or shady site
• Some flowers are fragrant

✿ **Houttuynia** (HOUTTUYNIA)
• Hardy, deciduous, perennials grown from rhizomes
• Aromatic leaves
• Moist potting mixture
• Semi-shady site
• Striking, colourful foliage

✿ **Hyacinthus** (HYACINTH)
• Hardy perennials grown from bulbs
• Dense spikes of fragrant, tubular, spring flowers
• Well-drained potting mixture
• Sunny or semi-shady site
• Bring planted bowls in to perfume the house in spring

✿ **Hydrangea** (HYDRANGEA)
• Hardy, deciduous shrubs or evergreen climbers
• Showy, summer flowers
• Rich, moist but well-drained potting mixture
• Sunny or semi-shady site
• Ideal for container culture

❋ Ilex (Holly)
- Hardy, deciduous or evergreen trees and shrubs
- Shiny foliage, and fruits
- Well-drained potting mixture
- Sunny or shady site
- Slow growing but can be trained as a topiary plant

❋ Impatiens (Busy Lizzie)
- Tender annuals and mainly evergreen perennials or sub-shrubs
- Summer flowers
- Moist but well-drained potting mixture
- Any site
- Long flowering season

❋ Juniperus (Juniper)
- Hardy conifers with scale- or needle-like foliage
- Year-round foliage, and berries
- Well-drained potting mixture
- Sunny site
- Will put up with extreme conditions

❋ Kalanchoe (Flaming Katy)
- Tender, perennial succulents or shrubs
- Fleshy leaves and bell- or tubular-shaped, spring flowers
- Well-drained potting mixture
- Sunny or semi-shady site
- Keep frost free and on the dry side throughout winter

❋ Lantana (Lantana)
- Tender, evergreen perennials, or shrubs or annuals
- Spring to autumn flowers
- Well-drained potting mixture
- Sunny or semi-shady site
- Prune out growing tips to promote bushy growth. Water freely during growing season

❋ Laurus (Bay)
- Hardy, evergreen trees
- Aromatic foliage
- Rich, well-drained potting mixture
- Sunny or semi-shady site
- Keep in sheltered position; water occasionally in winter

❋ Lavandula (Lavender)
- Hardy to half-hardy, evergreen shrubs
- Aromatic, grey-green leaves and summer flowers
- Rich, well-drained potting mixture
- Sunny site
- In milder areas, try the woolly-leaved, silvery Lavandula lanata

❋ Leucothöe (Leucothöe)
- Hardy, evergreen, semi-evergreen, or deciduous shrubs
- White, spring to summer flowers and attractive foliage

- Moist but well-drained, acid potting mixture
- Semi-shady or shady site
- Some new varieties have multi-coloured leaves

❋ Lewisia (Lewisia)
- Hardy to half-hardy perennials, some evergreen
- Summer flowers and rosettes of succulent leaves
- Well-drained potting mixture
- Sunny or semi-shady site
- Protect rosettes from damp during the winter months

❋ Ligustrum (Privet)
- Hardy, deciduous, semi-evergreen, or evergreen shrubs and trees
- Glossy leaves
- Well-drained potting mixture
- Sunny or semi-shady site
- Handsome container plants

❋ Lilium (Lily)
- Hardy perennials grown from bulbs
- Summer flowers
- Well-drained potting mixture
- Semi-shady site
- Regale lilies are the easiest to grow

❋ Lithodora (Lithodora)
- Hardy, evergreen sub-shrubs or shrubs
- Spring to summer flowers
- Moist but well-drained, lime-free potting mixture
- Sunny or semi-shady site
- Intense blue flowers

❋ Lobelia (Lobelia)
- Hardy to tender annuals, perennials, or deciduous or evergreen shrubs
- Spring to summer flowers
- Moist but well-drained potting mixture
- Sunny or semi-shady site
- Do not allow annuals to become too dry in summer

❋ Lobularia (Alyssum)
- Hardy annuals
- Tiny, summer and early autumn flowers
- Well-drained potting mixture
- Sunny site
- Deadhead regularly

❋ Lonicera (Honeysuckle)
- Hardy to tender, deciduous, semi-evergreen, or evergreen shrubs and climbers
- Fragrant, summer flowers
- Any rich, well-drained potting mixture
- Sunny or shady site
- Grow climbers up trellis from large pot

❋ Lotus berthelotii (Lotus)
- Tender perennials, some semi-evergreen
- Silver foliage and summer flowers

- Well-drained potting mixture
- Sunny site
- A trailing plant, ideal for hanging baskets

❋ Malvastrum lateritium (Malvastrum)
- Creeping perennials
- Profusion of summer and autumn flowers
- Well-drained, acid potting mixture with sand
- Sunny site
- Flowers are pale pink with brick-coloured centres

❋ Mimulus (Monkey flower)
- Hardy to half-hardy annuals and perennials
- Snapdragon-like, summer flowers
- Moist potting mixture
- Sunny site
- Keep damp and deadhead frequently for long display

❋ Muscari (Grape hyacinth)
- Hardy perennials grown from bulbs
- Spikes of small flowers
- Well-drained potting mixture
- Any site
- The blue or white flowers are buttery scented

❋ Myosotis (Forget-me-not)
- Hardy annuals, biennials, or perennials
- Spring flowers
- Rich, well-drained potting mixture
- Sunny or semi-shady site
- Blue flowers fade to pink

❋ Nandina domestica (Sacred bamboo)
- Hardy, evergreen or semi-evergreen shrubs
- Attractive foliage
- Rich, well-drained potting mixture
- Sunny site
- Young foliage is purple-red in autumn

❋ Narcissus (Daffodil)
- Hardy perennials grown from bulbs
- Spring flowers
- Well-drained potting mixture
- Sunny or semi-shady site
- Numerous varieties, mostly yellows and whites

❋ Nerine (Nerine)
- Hardy to half-hardy perennials grown from bulbs
- Waxy, pink, autumn flowers
- Light, sandy potting mixture
- Sunny site
- Roots dislike disturbance

❋ Nicotiana (Tobacco plant)
- Hardy to tender annuals, and perennials grown as annuals

- Long-lasting, mostly scented flowers
- Rich, well-drained potting mixture
- Semi-shady or shady site
- Some varieties are more fragrant than others

❋ Nymphaea pygmaea (Water lily)
- Hardy to tender, deciduous, perennial, floating aquatics
- Glossy leaves and striking, summer flowers
- Sunny site
- Remove fading foliage to prevent it polluting the water

❋ Papaver (Poppy)
- Hardy annuals, biennials, and perennials, some evergreen
- Colourful, summer flowers
- Moist, well-drained potting mixture
- Sunny or semi-shady site
- Alpine varieties do very well in sink gardens

❋ Pelargonium (Pelargonium)
- Tender perennials, mostly evergreen, often cultivated as annuals
- Summer flowers and attractive leaves, sometimes scented
- Well-drained potting mixture
- Sunny site
- Take softwood cuttings in late summer

❋ Pentas lanceolata (Pentas)
- Tender, evergreen perennials and shrubs
- Summer flowers
- Rich, well-drained potting mixture
- Sunny or semi-shady site
- Some varieties have white and pink flowers

❋ Pernettya (Pernettya)
- Hardy, evergreen shrubs
- Showy, long-lasting, autumn fruits
- Moist but well-drained, acid potting mixture
- Sunny or semi-shady site
- Requires male and female plants to produce berries

❋ Petunia (Petunia)
- Tender, bushy perennials grown as annuals
- Summer to autumn flowers
- Well-drained potting mixture
- Sheltered, sunny or semi-shady site
- Some varieties are sweetly scented

❋ Phormium (New Zealand flax)
- Hardy, evergreen perennials
- Bold, sword-shaped leaves
- Moist but well-drained potting mixture

- Sunny or semi-shady site
- Many varieties with striped and multi-coloured leaves

❋ Phyllostachys nigra (Black bamboo)
- Hardy, evergreen, clump-forming bamboo
- Attractive stems and leaves
- Well-drained potting mixture
- Sunny or semi-shady site
- The canes turn black in their second year

❋ Picea (Spruce)
- Hardy conifers with scale- or needle-like foliage
- Year-round foliage
- Well-drained potting mixture
- Sunny site
- Many species with blue, silver, or gold foliage

❋ Pieris (Pieris)
- Hardy, evergreen shrubs
- Colourful foliage and small, urn-shaped, spring flowers
- Moist, acid potting mixture
- Sheltered, semi-shady site
- New foliage is pink in spring

❋ Pinus (Pine)
- Hardy conifers with scale- or needle-like foliage
- Year-round foliage
- Well-drained potting mixture
- Sunny site
- Several species are ideal for exposed sites, tolerating wind and cold

❋ Plecostachys (Plecostachys)
- Half-hardy, evergreen sub-shrub
- Attractive silver foliage
- Well-drained potting mixture
- Sunny site
- Useful trailing foliage plant for the front of containers

❋ Plectranthus (Plectranthus)
- Tender, evergreen, trailing or bushy perennials
- Attractive foliage
- Moist potting mixture
- Sunny or semi-shady site
- Cut back tips in the growing season to prevent straggly growth

❋ Plumbago (Plumbago)
- Half-hardy to tender annuals, evergreen or semi-evergreen shrubs, perennials, or woody-stemmed, scrambling climbers
- Primrose-shaped, summer flowers, some of which are scented
- Well-drained potting mixture
- Sunny site
- Tie stems to supports and thin out previous year's growth in spring

❋ *Pogonatherum paniceum* (POGONATHERUM)
- Half-hardy, evergreen, clump-forming grass
- Low-growing thickets of leafy grass
- Well-drained potting mixture
- Sunny or semi-shady site
- Decorative, bamboo-like plant

❋ *Polygonatum x hybridum* (SOLOMON'S SEAL)
- Hardy perennials grown from rhizomes
- Spring or early summer flowers
- Rich, well-drained potting mixture
- Semi-shady or shady site
- Propagate by division in early spring

❋ *Polygonum* (POLYGONUM)
- Hardy annuals, perennials, some evergreen, and deciduous climbers
- Spikes of summer flowers
- Moist but well-drained potting mixture
- Sunny or shady site
- The leaves turn bronze in autumn and winter

❋ *Polypodium* (COMMON POLYPODY)
- Hardy, deciduous, semi-evergreen, or evergreen ferns
- Sculptural fronds
- Moist but well-drained potting mixture with leafmould
- Semi-shady site
- Decorative and easy to cultivate

❋ *Portulaca* (PORTULACA)
- Half-hardy, fleshy annuals and perennials
- Colourful, summer flowers
- Well-drained potting mixture
- Sunny or semi-shady site
- Flowers open only when the sun is out

❋ *Potentilla* (POTENTILLA)
- Hardy perennials and deciduous shrubs
- Saucer-shaped, summer flowers
- Well-drained potting mixture
- Sunny site
- Profuse yellow, orange, pink, and white flowers over a long period

❋ *Primula* (PRIMULA)
- Hardy to tender annuals, biennials, or perennials, some of which are evergreen
- Attractive, spring flowers, produced in large umbels on stout stems
- Well-drained potting mixture
- Sunny or semi-shady site
- Varieties offer an enormous range of colours

❋ *Pulsatilla vulgaris* (PASQUE FLOWER)
- Hardy perennials, some evergreen
- Upright or pendent, bell- or cup-shaped, spring flowers
- Well-drained potting mixture with leafmould
- Sunny site
- Dislike root disturbance

❋ *Ranunculus asiaticus* (PERSIAN BUTTERCUP)
- Hardy to half-hardy perennials grown from tubers
- Late spring flowers
- Moist but well drained potting mixture
- Sunny or semi-shady site
- Overwinter in frost-free site

❋ *Rhododendron* (AZALEA/RHODODENDRON)
- Hardy, evergreen, semi-evergreen, or deciduous shrubs
- Showy, spring flowers, and sometimes, autumn foliage
- Rich, well-drained, acid potting mixture with leafmould
- Semi-shady or shady site
- All but the largest species do well in containers

❋ *Rosa* (ROSE)
- Hardy, deciduous or semi-evergreen shrubs and climbers
- Fragrant flowers and autumn rosehips
- Rich, moist but well-drained potting mixture
- Sunny site
- Lower-growing, bushy varieties are best for growing in containers

❋ *Rosmarinus* (ROSEMARY)
- Hardy evergreen shrubs
- Aromatic foliage and spring flowers
- Well-drained potting mixture
- Sunny site
- Place pots where you can brush against the foliage to release the fragrance

❋ *Salvia* (SAGE)
- Hardy to tender annuals, biennials, perennials, or evergreen or semi-evergreen shrubs or sub-shrubs
- Spikes of summer to autumn flowers and coloured foliage
- Well-drained potting mixture
- Sunny site
- Some species have aromatic foliage

❋ *Santolina* (SANTOLINA)
- Hardy, evergreen shrubs
- Aromatic, silver foliage and yellow, summer flowers
- Well-drained potting mixture
- Sunny site
- Good species for providing year-round interest

❋ *Saxifraga paniculata* AND *S. longifolia* (SAXIFRAGE)
- Hardy to half-hardy perennials, mostly evergreen or semi-evergreen
- Rosette form and spring to summer flowers
- Well-drained, alkaline potting mixture
- Sunny site
- Good for growing in troughs and sinks

❋ *Scabiosa* (SCABIOUS)
- Hardy annuals and perennials, some evergreen
- Pincushion-like, summer flowers
- Rich, well-drained, alkaline potting mixture
- Sunny site
- Some species are scented

❋ *Scilla* (SQUILL)
- Hardy to half-hardy perennials grown from bulbs
- Spikes of small, often blue, spring flowers
- Well-drained potting mixture
- Sunny or semi-shady site
- Bring pots inside to flower

❋ *Sedum* (STONECROP)
- Hardy to tender, often fleshy or succulent annuals, evergreen biennials, or mostly evergreen perennials
- Attractive foliage and summer to autumn flowers
- Well-drained potting mixture
- Sunny site
- Needs only a little potting mixture in which to grow

❋ *Sempervivum* (HOUSELEEK)
- Hardy, spreading, evergreen perennials
- Rosettes of fleshy leaves and summer flowers
- Well-drained potting mixture with fine gravel
- Sunny site
- Needs only a little potting mixture in which to grow

❋ *Senecio* (SENECIO)
- Hardy to tender annuals, succulent or non-succulent perennials, or evergreen shrubs and sub-shrubs
- Attractive foliage and, usually, daisy-like, spring to autumn flowers
- Well-drained potting mixture
- Sunny or semi-shady site
- A silver-leaved species

❋ *Skimmia* (SKIMMIA)
- Hardy, evergreen shrubs or trees
- Spring flowers, aromatic foliage, and colourful autumn fruits
- Moisture-retentive potting mixture
- Semi-shady or shady site
- Grow near the house to appreciate their sweet-scented flowers

❋ *Solanum capsicastrum* (WINTER CHERRY)
- Hardy to tender, evergreen sub-shrubs
- Glossy foliage and ornamental, winter fruits
- Well-drained potting mixture
- Sunny site
- Useful winter-interest plant

❋ *Tagetes* (MARIGOLD)
- Half-hardy annuals
- Bright summer to autumn flowers
- Well-drained potting mixture
- Sunny site
- Flowers over a long period

❋ *Taxus* (YEW)
- Hardy conifers with scale- or needle-like foliage
- Year-round, ornamental foliage
- Well-drained potting mixture
- Any site
- Berries are poisonous

❋ *Thuja* (THUJA)
- Hardy conifers with scale- or needle-like foliage
- All-year ornamental foliage
- Well-drained potting mixture
- Any site
- Leaves have a fruity scent

❋ *Thunbergia alata* (BLACK-EYED SUSAN)
- Half-hardy to tender, fast-growing, annual climbers
- Small, orange-yellow, summer flowers
- Rich, well-drained potting mixture
- Sunny or semi-shady site
- Plant out late to avoid frost

❋ *Thymus* (THYME)
- Hardy to half-hardy, evergreen shrubs and sub-shrubs
- Aromatic foliage
- Moist but well-drained potting mixture
- Sunny site
- Grow near the kitchen

❋ *Tolmiea* (PICK-A-BACK PLANT)
- Hardy perennials that are sometimes semi-evergreen
- Attractive foliage
- Well-drained, neutral to acid potting mixture
- Semi-shady or shady site
- Propagate by removing plantlets

❋ *Tradescantia* (WANDERING JEW)
- Hardy to tender perennials, some evergreen
- Trailing habit and decorative foliage
- Rich, well-drained potting mixture
- Sunny or semi-shady site
- House plants that do well outside in summer

❋ *Tropaeolum majus* (NASTURTIUM)
- Hardy to tender annuals, perennials, or climbers
- Bright, summer flowers
- Well-drained potting mixture
- Sunny site
- Aphids can be a problem

❋ *Tulipa* (TULIP)
- Hardy perennials grown from bulbs
- Colourful, spring flowers
- Well-drained, preferably alkaline, potting mixture
- Sunny or semi-shady site
- Available in a wide range of sizes, colours, and forms

❋ *Verbena* (VERBENA)
- Hardy to tender perennials, and biennials grown as annuals
- Colourful, summer flowers
- Well-drained potting mixture
- Sunny or semi-shady site
- Some have scented flowers

❋ *Vinca* (PERIWINKLE)
- Hardy, evergreen, trailing sub-shrubs or perennials
- Decorative foliage and intermittent spring to autumn flowers
- Well-drained potting mixture
- Any site
- Flowers more in sunny sites

❋ *Viola* (PANSY)
- Hardy to half-hardy annuals, and perennials, some semi-evergreen
- Different varieties flower all year
- Well-drained, moisture-retentive potting mixture
- Any site
- Deadhead to encourage flowering

❋ *Weigela* (WEIGELA)
- Hardy, deciduous shrubs
- Showy, spring to summer flowers and attractive foliage
- Rich potting mixture
- Sunny site
- Coloured and variegated varieties are available

❋ *Yucca* (YUCCA)
- Hardy to tender, evergreen shrubs or trees
- Bold, sword-shaped leaves and showy panicles of summer flowers
- Well-drained potting mixture
- Sunny or semi-shady site
- Hardier than is supposed

❋ *Zinnia* (ZINNIA)
- Half-hardy annuals
- Large, dahlia-like, summer flowers
- Rich, well-drained potting mixture
- Sunny site
- Striped- and splashed-flowered varieties available

INDEX

A

Abelia x *grandiflora*, 26
Abutilon, 85, 112, 184
   A. x *hybridum* 'Golden Fleece', 46-7
Acer (maples), 129, 137, 184
   A. negundo variegata, 133
   A. palmatum, 121, 144
Achillea millefolium, 136, 137
acid soils, 24, 78, 118
Adiantum capillus-veneris (maidenhair fern), 118, 123, 126, 184
Agapanthus, 11, 139, 184
   A. campanulatus (African lily), 112, 113
agave, 107, 137, 184
Ageratum (floss flower), 112, 184
   A. 'Bengali', 66
   A. houstonianum 'Blue Mink', 155
Agrostemma (corn cockle), 112
Ajuga (bugle), 136
Alchemilla mollis (lady's mantle), 113
alkaline soils, 118
Allium (onions), 113
   A. schoenoprasum (chives), 168
aloe, 107, 137, 184
alpine plants, 85, 87, 131, 134, 158-9
alpine poppies (*Papaver burseri*), 158
alyssum (*Lobularia maritima*), 61, 66, 94, 107, 110, 113, 121, 155, 163, 186
Amaranthus, 137
   A. caudatus, 136
Anemone (windflowers), 112, 120
   A. blanda 'White Splendour', 101, 184
   A. x *hybrida* (Japanese anemone), 129
angelica, 169
angels' trumpets (*Datura arborea*), 140
annuals, 11
   deadheading, 181
   foliage, 22-3
   raising from seed, 182
Anthemis (chamomile)
   A. punctata cupaniana, 87, 107, 110, 112, 184

Antirrhinum (snapdragon), 47, 66, 96, 107, 110, 113, 134, 137, 163, 177, 184
   A. majus, 137
   A.m. 'Trumpet Serenade', 163
   A. pulverulentum, 47
   A. 'Sweetheart', 96
aphids, 176, 177
apple trees, 107
Aquilegia (columbine), 121, 184
   A. vulgaris 'Nora Barlow', 120
Artemisia (southernwood), 113, 136, 184
   A. abrotanum, 21, 107, 115
arum lily (*Zantedeschia* hybrid), 121
asparagus, 112, 121, 184
asparagus fern, 118
Aspidistra, 184
   A. elatior, 116, 123
Aster (Michaelmas daisy), 11, 112, 121, 126, 184
   A. novi-belgii Dwarf form, 56
Astilbe, 105, 121, 184
   A. x *arendsii*, 121
Astrantia (masterwort), 121
aubrieta, 8, 38, 136
aucuba, 110, 120, 123, 126, 128
auricula (*Primula auricula*), 28-9, 112, 120
autumn crocus (*Colchicum*), 137, 187
azaleas, 40-1, 118, 120, 128

B

bamboo, 120, 123, 126, 128, 131, 133, 186
barrels, 74-83
basil, purple, 169
baskets: hanging, 93-5, 102-3
   moss, 102-3
   planting, 154-5
   wall, 93, 98-9
   watering, 180
bay *see Laurus nobilis*
bayberry (*Myrica pensylvanica*), 136
Begonia, 54-5, 61, 66-7, 72, 93, 94, 105, 123, 126, 129, 177, 183, 184
   B. 'Norah Bedson', 53
   B. rex 'Merry Christmas', 53

   B. semperflorens, 154
   B. x *tuberhybrida*, 22-3, 54, 116-17, 118, 124, 128, 129
      B. x *t.* 'Billie Langdon', 53
      B. x *t. pendula*, 55, 124
      B. x *t.* 'Roy Hartley', 99
bellflowers *see Campanula*
Bellis perennis (daisy), 101, 112, 184
bergamot (*Monarda*), 137
Bergenia, 120, 123, 128
   B. 'Ballawley', 62
berries, 26, 58-9
black-eyed Susan (*Thunbergia alata*), 69, 112, 187
blackfly, 177
blechnum, 123
bleeding heart (*Dicentra spectabilis*), 120, 121
blue spruce (*Picea pungens* 'Glauca'), 77
blueberries (*Vaccinium*), 83, 136
Boston ferns (*Nephrolepis exaltata* 'Bostoniensis'), 170
box *see Buxus*
Brachycome (rain daisy), 140
Brassica oleracea (ornamental cabbage), 26, 113, 165, 184
broom (*Cytisus*), 36-7, 70, 112, 185
buckets, mop, 160-1
bugle (*Ajuga*), 136
bulbs: in exposed sites, 131, 134
   planting and layering, 34
   in shady sites, 126
   in stone sinks, 86-7
   in tubs, 75
busy Lizzies *see Impatiens*
Buxus (box), 184
   B. sempervirens, 6, 26
   locations, 110, 113, 115, 120, 123, 124, 126, 128, 131, 136
   standards, 59, 108
   topiary, 149, 166

C

cabbage, ornamental (*Brassica oleracea*), 26, 113, 184
cacti, 107, 123
Calceolaria, 94, 112, 184

   C. 'Sunshine', 95
Calendula (marigolds), 137, 184
Californian bluebells, 61
Calluna (heather), 184
   C. vulgaris, 24-5, 113, 121
camellias, 118, 120, 123, 126, 150, 177, 181, 182, 183, 184
Campanula (bellflowers), 20, 61, 90, 115, 121, 123, 129, 184
   C. carpatica, 50
   C. cochleariifolia (fairy thimbles), 159
   C. garganica, 86
ceanothus, 64
Celosia, 184
   C. cristata, 112, 161
Centaurea (cornflower), 137
Centranthus (valerian), 137
ceramic containers, 26, 36-7, 64-5 *see also* terracotta
Ceratostigma, 113, 137, 184
   C. plumbaginoides, 57
cereus, 107
Chamaecyparis lawsoniana (Lawson cypress), 166, 184
   C.l. 'Nana Glauca', 24-5
chamomile (*Anthemis punctata cupaniana*), 87, 107, 110, 112, 184
chard, ruby, 169
Cheiranthus (wallflowers), 112, 184
   C. cheiri, 116
   C. 'Rufus', 136
cherry: flowering (*Prunus*), 112
   winter (*Solanum capsicastrum*), 26
cherry pie (*Heliotropium peruvianum*), 16-17, 112, 140
chimney pots, 156-7
Chionodoxa (glory-of-the-snow), 112
chives (*Allium schoenoprasum*), 168
Chlorophytum (spider plant), 126, 184
Choisya ternata (Mexican orange blossom), 120, 121, 126, 181, 184
   C.t. 'Aztec Pearl', 118
   C.t. 'Sundance', 27, 118
Christmas rose (*Helleborus niger*), 30

Chrysanthemum, 11, 18-19, 66, 71, 112, 113, 121, 137, 176, 177, 184
   'trees', 59
   C. 'Dawn Mist', 59
   C. frutescens, 8, 20-1, 61, 85
   C. parthenium 'Aureum' (golden feverfew), 18-19, 71
chusan palms, 123
cigar flower (*Cuphea ignea*), 61, 112, 185
cineraria *see Senecio*
Cistus (rock roses), 64, 113
clam shells, 86-7
Clarkia (godetia), 112
cleaning containers, 178-9
climbers: pergolas, 108-9, 140
   supports, 172
   topiary, 166, 167
   clipping, 25, 166
clivia, 123
Colchicum (autumn crocus), 137
cold weather, 26
Coleus blumei, 22-3, 97, 108, 112, 121, 131, 161, 182, 183, 184
colour: coordinating flowers and containers, 65
   exposed sites, 131
   in low bowls, 61
   semi-shady sites, 115
   shady sites, 126
   sunny sites, 107, 110
   window boxes, 15
columbine (*Aquilegia vulgaris*), 115, 121, 176, 184
conifers, 132, 144
   foliage, 26
   locations, 113, 120, 128, 134
   miniature hedges, 25
   planting, 76
   topiary, 166
Convallaria majalis (lily-of-the-valley), 86, 120, 128, 129, 184
Convolvulus, 61, 64, 94
   C. cneorum, 112
coppers, 61, 160
Cordyline, 107, 137, 178, 185
   C. australis, 132
corn cockle (*Agrostemma*), 112
cornflower (*Centaurea*), 137
cotinus, 137

Cotoneaster, 26, 121, 136, 134, 185
courgettes, 83, 112
courtyards, 116-17
cowslip (*Primula veris*), 86-7, 112
cranesbills (*Geranium*), 61, 115, 123, 185
creeping Jenny, 61
crocks, bread, 82
crocuses, 34, 110, 112, 113, 136, 185
crown imperials (*Fritillaria imperialis*), 38-9, 112, 120, 185
Cuphea ignea (cigar flower), 61, 112, 185
Cupressocyparis leylandii 'Castlewellan', 166
Cupressus , 185
 C. arizonica, 136
 C. macrocarpa, 136
curry plant (*Helichrysum italicum*), 90-1, 113
cuttings, 182, 183
Cyclamen, 121, 129, 185
 C. hederifolium var. *album,* 165
cypresses, 24-5, 136, 185
 false, 26
 Lawson (*Chamaecyparis lawsoniana*), 24-5, 166
Cytisus (broom), 112, 185
 C. 'Cornish Cream', 70
 C. x *spachianus,* 36-7

daffodils *see Narcissus*
Dahlia, 13, 66, 113, 137, 176, 185
 D. 'Fascination', 136
 D. 'Redskin', 162-3
daisies (*Bellis perennis*), 101, 112, 184
Daphne mezereum, 113
Datura, 9
 D. arborea (angels' trumpets), 140
deadheading, 181
Delphinium elatum 'Sungleam', 112
Dianthus (pinks), 15, 61, 107, 185
 D. 'Little Jock', 87
 D. 'Monica Wyatt', 137
Diascia, 69, 112, 185
 D. rigescens, 52
Dicentra spectabilis (bleeding heart), 120, 121
diseases and pests, 176-7
division, 182
dog's tooth violets (*Erythronium*), 86-7, 128, 185
doorways, 139, 144-5
drainage, 178

drought, 134
Dryopteris, 185
 D. erythrosora (Japanese shield fern), 129
 D. filix-mas (male fern), 117

E

earwigs, 176
echeverias, 107, 137, 139, 185
Eichhornia acicularis (water hyacinth), 110
Elaeagnus, 110, 123, 134, 136, 185
 E. ebbingei, 129
epiphyllum cactus, 123
Eranthis hyemalis (winter aconite), 113
Erica (heather), 113, 185
 E. carnea 'Springwood White', 90-1
 E. x *darleyensis,* 24
 E. vagans, 26
Erythronium (dog's tooth violet), 185
 E. 'Pagoda', 86-7, 128
Euonymus, 10, 110, 120, 123, 126, 134, 185
 E. angustifolius, 26
 E. fortunei, 113, 136
  E.f. 'Emerald 'n' Gold', 27, 101
  E.f. 'Silver Queen', 137
  E.f. 'Sunspot', 137
 E. japonicus, 136
Euphorbia (spurge), 112, 113, 136, 185
 E. myrsinites, 101
Eustoma, 185
 E. grandiflorum, 108-9, 112, 144
evening gardens, 150-1
evergreens: pruning, 181
 shady sites, 123
 standard plants, 59
 in winter, 11, 26-7, 110
everlasting flower (*Helichrysum bracteatum*), 161
exposed sites, 130-7

F

fairy thimbles (*Campanula cochleariifolia*), 159
Fatsia, 110, 120, 123, 128
 F. japonica, 129, 185
felicia, 94
fences, 146
ferns, 85, 87, 115, 117, 123, 128
fertilizers, 180
feverfew, golden (*Chrysanthemum parthenium* 'Aureum'), 18-19, 71

fibreglass containers, 15, 75, 85, 146
Ficus pumila (creeping fig), 121, 126, 129, 166, 185
flaming Katy (*Kalanchoe blossfeldiana*), 86-7, 112, 186
flax (*Phormium cookianum* 'Variegatum'), 133, 186
floss flowers (*Ageratum*), 66, 112, 155, 184
focal points, 139
foliage, 11
 annuals, 22-3
 aromatic, 107
 conifers, 76
 evergreens, 26-7
 in shady sites, 123
 pelargoniums, 48-9
 perennial plants, 51
 silver, 20-1
forget-me-not (*Myosotis*), 38, 112, 120, 186
fragrance *see* scent
French marigolds (*Tagetes*), 112, 131, 161
Fritillaria imperialis (crown imperial), 38-9, 112, 120, 185
 F. meleagris (snake's head fritillary), 86-7, 120, 128, 185
frost, 26, 56
fruit, 83, 107
Fuchsia, 8, 10, 54-5, 59, 64, 66, 72, 78, 121, 123,126, 129, 140, 144, 185
 F. 'Annabel', 157
 F. 'Autumnale', 116-17
 F. 'Citation', 171
 F. 'Gruss aus dem Bodenthal', 99
 F. 'Mrs Popple', 118
 F. 'Pink Galore', 99, 120
 F. 'Thalia', 55, 118, 125
fungal infections, 177

gaultheria, 120, 123, 128, 185
Gazania, 107, 112, 185
 G. 'Daybreak', 72
 G. uniflora, 18-19
Gentiana verna (spring gentian), 112
Geranium (cranesbills), 185
 G. endressii, 61
 G. nodosum, 61
 G. palmatum, 140
gladiolus, 113
Gleditsia (locust), 137, 185
 G. triacanthos 'Sunburst', 132
glory-of-the-snow (*Chionodoxa*), 112
godetia (*Clarkia*), 112

gorse (*Ulex*), 136
grape hyacinths (*Muscari*), 8, 36, 63, 112, 120, 136, 186
greenfly, 177
grouping containers, 33, 56-7
Gypsophila, 112
 G. repens 'Dorothy Teacher', 46

H

X *Halimiocistus* (sun roses), 112, 185
 X *H. wintonensis* 'Merrist Wood Cream', 64-5
hanging baskets, 93-103, 180
hayracks, 98-9
heather, 24-5, 64, 90-1, 113, 121, 184, 185
Hebe, 64, 113, 185
 H. 'Lindsayi', 57
 H. pinguifolia 'Pagei', 90-91
Hedera (ivy), 10, 26, 61, 72, 75, 108, 123, 126, 131, 166, 167, 185
 H. 'Buttercup', 61
 H. 'Eva', 86
 H. helix, 96, 113, 120, 128
  H.h. 'Dealbata', 118
  H.h. 'Deltoidea', 167
  H.h. 'Duck's Foot', 86, 129
  H.h. 'Elegance', 25
  H.h. 'Eva', 117
  H.h. 'Gracilis', 155
  H.h. 'Ivalace', 90-1
  H.h. 'Parsley Crested', 36-7
  H.h. 'Pittsburgh', 79
  H.h. 'Sagittifolia Variegata', 77, 144
  H.h. 'Telecurl', 70
 H. 'Ivalace', 86
 H. 'Manda's Crested', 86
helenium, 137
Helichrysum, 9, 85, 107, 112, 185
 H. bracteatum Monstrosum Series (everlasting flower), 161
 H. italicum (curry plant), 90-1, 113
 H. petiolare, 21, 94-5, 140, 172
  H.p. aureum, 96
Heliotropium (heliotrope), 185
 H. peruvianum , 16-17, 112, 140
Helleborus, 120, 128, 185
 H. niger (Christmas rose), 30, 120, 128
 H. orientalis (Lenten rose), 30

 H. x *sternii,* 30-1, 121
hemlock, 126
herbs, 139, 168-9
Heuchera, 121, 185
 H. 'Palace Purple', 51, 123
 H. 'Snowstorm', 87
hibiscus, 107
holly (*Ilex*), 123, 126, 136, 186
holly fern (*Phanerophlebia falcata*), 117, 123
honeysuckles (*Lonicera*), 9, 123, 128, 129, 172, 186
Hosta, 9, 121, 129, 144, 182
 H. sieboldiana, 128
  H.s. 'Frances Williams', 116
houseleeks (*Sempervivum*), 61, 85, 112, 137, 187
Houttuynia, 113, 121, 185
 H. cordata 'Chamaeleon', 51, 56, 112
Hyacinthus (hyacinths), 34, 110, 112, 136, 140, 185
 H. orientalis, 120
  H.o. 'Oranje Boven', 28
Hydrangea, 121, 123, 139, 181, 185
 H. macrophylla, 129
  H.m. 'Hamburg', 171
Hypericum (St John's wort), 129

iberis, 136, 186
ice plant (*Sedum spectabile*), 137
Ilex (holly), 26, 123, 126, 136
Impatiens (busy Lizzies), 20, 66, 93, 94, 116, 117, 118, 121, 123, 126, 129, 150, 182, 183, 186
 I. New Guinea hybrid, 67, 78, 99, 108-9, 120
 I. walleriana, 117, 118, 144, 150
  I.w. 'Tangeglow', 116
Iris, 75, 112, 136
 I. unguicularis, 113
ivy *see Hedera*

J

Japanese anemones (*Anemone* x *hybrida*), 129
Japanese honeysuckle (*Lonicera japonica* 'Halliana'), 172
Japanese maples (*Acer palmatum*), 121
Japanese shield ferns (*Dryopteris erythrosora*), 129
jars, 68-73
Jasminum (jasmine), 9, 129

Juniperus (junipers), 76, 132, 136, 186
J. conferta, 26-7
J. horizontalis 'Bar Harbor', 91
J. sabina 'Tamariscifolia', 133

K

Kaffir lilies (*Schizostylis*), 113, 137
Kalanchoe blossfeldiana (flaming Katy), 86-7, 112, 186
Kirengeshoma palmata, 129

L

laburnum, 176
lady's mantle (*Alchemilla mollis*), 113
Lantana, 94, 112, 186
L. camara, 71, 72-3
Lathyrus (sweet peas), 113
Laurus (bay), 186
L. nobilis, 6, 59, 108, 132, 136, 140, 144, 166, 168, 177
laurustinus (*Viburnum tinus*), 120
Lavandula (lavender), 186
L. angustifolia, 8, 26, 61, 64, 107, 112, 115, 134, 136, 144
L. lanata, 113
Lavatera (mallow), 113
L. 'Mont Blanc', 72
lavender *see Lavandula*
Lawson cypress (*Chamaecyparis lawsoniana*), 24-5, 184
layering, propagation, 182
layering bulbs, 34
leaf bud cuttings, 183
leaf miners, 176
lemon balm, 107
lemon verbena, 107, 142
Lenten rose (*Helleborus orientalis*), 30
Leucothoë, 120, 126, 128, 186
L. fontanesiana 'Rainbow', 51
L. 'Scarletta', 62
Lewisia, 87, 121, 186
L. 'Cotyledon hybrid', 159
lichen, 31, 38
Ligustrum (privet), 186
L. 'Vicaryi', 26
L. vulgare 'Buxifolium', 144, 149
lilac, 176
Lilium (lilies), 8, 50, 121, 140, 150, 186
L. 'Casa Blanca', 150
L. 'Connecticut King', 50
L. 'La Reve', 121, 150

L. regale, 150
lily-of-the-valley (*Convallaria majalis*), 86, 120, 128, 129, 184
Limonium sinuatum (statice), 137
liriope, 137
Lithodora, 186
L. diffusa 'Heavenly Blue', 86
Livingstone daisy (*Mesembryanthemum*), 112, 137
Lobelia, 10, 61, 66, 93, 94, 110, 113, 121, 123, 142, 186
L. erinus 'Cascade Mixture', 95
L.e. 'White Cascade', 156-7
Lobularia (alyssum), 186
L. maritima, 113, 121
L.m. 'Little Dorrit', 94, 155
L.m. 'Wonderland', 163
locust (*Gleditsia*), 132, 137, 185
Lonicera (honeysuckle), 129, 186
L. japonica 'Halliana' (Japanese honeysuckle), 128, 172
loosestrife (*Lysimachia*), 121
Lotus, 94
L. berthelotii, 97, 108-9, 113, 186
louse, 176
Lysimachia (loosestrife), 121

M

Madonna lilies, 150
magnolias, 183
Mahonia, 123, 126, 128, 177
M. lomariifolia, 129
maidenhair fern (*Adiantum capillus-veneris*), 123, 126, 184
male fern (*Dryopteris felix-mas*), 117, 185
mallow (*Lavatera*), 113
malvastrum, 13, 186
maples (*Acer*), 121, 129, 133, 137, 144, 184
Maranta leuconeura, 113
marguerites, 8, 20-1, 61, 85, 144
marigolds, 47, 61, 66, 107, 110, 112, 131, 134, 137, 161, 184, 187
marjoram (*Origanum vulgare*), 18-19, 113, 169
marvel of Peru, 140
masterwort (*Astrantia*), 121

Matthiola (stocks), 113
Mentha x *gentilis* 'Variegata' (variegated mint), 169
Mesembryanthemum (Livingstone daisy), 112, 137
Mexican orange blossom (*Choisya ternata*), 27, 118, 120, 121, 123, 181, 184
Michaelmas daisies (*Aster*), 112, 121, 184
mignonette, 107
mildew, 177
Mimulus (monkey flower), 113, 121, 129, 186
M. aurantiacus, 149
mint, 168, 169
Mirabilis jalopa (marvel of Peru), 140
Monarda (bergamot), 137
monkey flower (*Mimulus*), 113, 121, 129, 149
mop buckets, 160-1
mop-heads, 170-1
moss: baskets, 93, 102-3
covering bulbs with, 35
herb towers, 168
topiary forms, 167
weathering terracotta, 31, 38
woodland gardens, 86-7
mountain pines (*Pinus mugo*), 132
Muscari (grape hyacinths), 8, 36, 112, 120, 136, 186
M. azureum, 63
M. botryoides 'Album', 63
Myosotis (forget-me-not), 112, 120, 186
M. 'Blue Ball', 38
Myrica pensylvanica (bayberry), 136
myrtle, 6

N

Nandina domestica (sacred bamboo), 133, 186
Narcissus (daffodils), 34, 36, 42, 75, 78, 102-3, 110, 112, 120, 128, 136, 140, 186
N. 'April Tears', 102-3
N. 'Salmon Trout', 42
N. 'Tahiti', 42
N. 'Tête-à-Tête', 42
N. 'Yellow Cheerfulness', 42
nasturtiums (*Tropaeolum*), 22-3, 52, 66, 94, 113, 134, 136, 137, 142, 149, 187
nemesia, 113
Nephrolepis exaltata 'Bostoniensis', 170
Nerine bowdenii, 113, 137, 186

New Zealand ferns, 123
New Zealand flax (*Phormium tenax*), 116-17, 137, 186
Nicotiana (tobacco plant), 8, 20, 54-5, 66, 78, 121, 123, 126, 129, 150, 186
N. alata, 142, 144, 150
N.a. Sensation Series, 55, 121
N. 'Pink Bedder', 124
N. sylvestris, 150
night-scented stocks, 8-9
Nymphaea (water lilies), 113
N. pygmaea 'Helvola', 110, 186

O

onions (*Allium*), 113
oregano, 168
Origanum (marjoram), 113
O. vulgare, 169
O.v. 'Aureum' (golden marjoram), 18-19
osmanthus, 123
Osmunda regalis, 128

P

Pachysandra, 123, 128, 136
P. terminalis, 129
pansies *see Viola*
Papaver (poppy), 113, 186
P. burseri (alpine poppy), 158
P. miyabeanum, 158
parsley (*Petroselinum crispum*), 113, 168, 169
pasque flowers (*Pulsatilla vulgaris*), 101, 112, 120, 187
paths, 148-9
pear trees, 107
peat, 178, 180
Pelargonium (geraniums), 10, 11, 13, 52, 146, 186
containers for, 66, 85, 94
cuttings, 183
deadheading, 181
locations, 110, 113, 121, 137, 140, 144
planting, 44
standards, 59, 171
variegated, 48-9
P. 'Appleblossom Rosebud', 109
P. 'Braque', 144
P. 'Deacon Bonanza', 170
P. 'Dolly Varden', 48-9
P. 'Elégante', 72, 162-3
P. 'Frank Headley', 49
P. 'Ivalo', 109
P. 'Lady Plymouth', 48-9
P. 'Madame Crousse', 95
P. 'Mauritania', 109
P. 'Mrs Quilter', 49

P. 'Modesty', 20-1
P. 'Rio', 109, 136
P. 'Tavira', 97
P. 'Tip Top Duet', 45
P. 'Yale', 97, 108, 136
Pentas, 113, 186
P. lanceolata, 72-3
pergolas, 108-9, 140
periwinkles (*Vinca*), 26, 63, 72, 120, 123, 128, 187
Pernettya, 186
P. mucronata, 113, 121
P.m. alba, 58
P.m. 'Bell's Seedling', 58
P.m. 'Edward Ball', 58
P.m. 'Mulberry Wine', 58
Persian buttercup (*Ranunculus asiaticus*), 36, 112, 120, 121, 186
pests and diseases, 176-7
Petroselinum crispum (parsley), 113, 168, 169
Petunia, 16-17, 20, 47, 52, 66, 72, 75, 85, 94, 107, 110, 137, 186
petunia wilt, 16, 176
P. x *hybrida*, 80-1, 113
P. x *h.* 'Red Satin', 22-3
P. Ruffles Series, 112, 113
Phanerophlebia falcata (holly fern), 117, 123
philodendron, 129
phlebodium, 123
Phlomis, 137
Phlox, 87, 107
P. subulata, 112
Phormium (flax), 186
P. cookianum 'Variegatum', 133
P. tenax (New Zealand flax), 137
P.t. 'Variegatum', 116-17
phylitis, 123
Phyllostachys nigra (black bamboo), 133, 186
Picea, 186
P. glauca albertiana 'Conica', 76, 133
P. pungens 'Glauca' (blue spruce), 77
pick-a-back plant (*Tolmiea menziesii*), 51, 61, 115, 121, 126, 129, 187
Pieris, 26, 120, 123, 128, 186
P. 'Flaming Silver', 78-9
P. floribunda, 136
pinks (*Dianthus*), 15, 61, 87, 107, 137, 185
Pinus (pine trees), 76, 132, 136, 186
P. mugo (mountain pine), 76, 132
P. wallichiana, 76
Pistia stratiotes (water lettuce), 110
planting, 178-9

baskets, 154-5
bulbs, 34
chimney pots, 156
conifers, 76
hanging baskets, 94
herbs, 168
mop buckets, 160-1
pelargoniums, 44
repotting, 178-9
topiary, 167
window boxes, 16
plastic window boxes, 15
Plecostachys, 69, 113, 186
P. serpyllifolia, 71
Plectranthus, 121, 186
P. coleoides 'Variegatus',
71
plum trees, 107
Plumbago, 113, 139, 186
P. auriculata, 39
polyantha roses *(Rosa
'Margot Koster')*, 109
polyanthus *(Primula*
hybrids), 28, 102-3, 112,
113
Pogonatherum paniceum,
126, 127
Polygonatum x *hybridum*
(Solomon's seal), 38,
120, 128, 187
Polygonum, 121, 187
P. affine 'Donald
Lowndes', 86
Polypodium (common
polypody), 187
P. vulgare, 87
Polystichum, 123
P. setiferum, 144
poppies *(Papaver)*, 113,
158, 186
porcelain sinks, 85, 158
porches, 140
Portulaca, 113, 137, 142,
187
P. grandiflora, 94-5
P. g. Sunnyside Series,
108
potentillas, 64, 113, 121,
134, 187
potting mixtures, 176, 178
prickly pear, 107
Primula, 113, 120, 128, 187
P. auricula, 28-9, 112, 120
P. Pacific hybrids
(polyanthus), 102-3
P. veris (cowslip), 86-7,
120
P. vulgaris (polyanthus),
28, 112
privet *(Ligustrum)*, 108, 110,
126, 144, 149, 166, 187
propagation, 182-3
pruning, 166, 181
Prunus (flowering cherry),
112
Prunus laurocerasus, 123
Pulsatilla vulgaris (pasque
flower), 101, 112, 120,
187

puschkinia, 136
pyracantha, 129

R

rain daisy, 140
Ranunculus asiaticus
(Persian buttercup), 36,
112, 120, 121, 187
repotting, 178-9
Rhododendron, 40-1, 75,
118, 120, 126, 128, 181,
183, 187
R. 'Fedora', 40
R. 'Grumpy', 116
R. 'Konigen Emma', 41
R. 'Nobleanum', 128
R. 'Vuyk's Scarlet', 41
Rhus (sumach), 137
rock plants (alpines), 85,
87, 131, 134, 158-9
rock roses *(Cistus)*, 64, 113
roof terraces, 131, 132-3
Rosa (roses), 11, 43, 75,
82, 107, 113, 121,
177, 181, 187
R. 'Ballerina', 108-9
R. 'The Fairy', 43, 113
R. 'Ferdinand Pichard', 82
R. 'Margot Koster', 109
R. 'New Dawn', 120
R. 'Robin Redbreast', 82
R. 'Stars 'n' Stripes', 82
R. 'Yellow Cushion', 43
Rosmarinus (rosemary), 187
R. officinalis, 107, 113,
115, 136, 168
R.o. 'Prostratus', 90-1
rue *(Ruta graveolens)*, 112,
121
rust, 177
rustic effects, 164
Ruta graveolens (rue), 112,
121

S

safety, window boxes, 15
sage *see Salvia*
St John's wort
(Hypericum), 129
Salvia (sage), 107, 110,
113, 136, 140, 187
S. officinalis, 136
S.o. 'Purpurascens'
(purple sage), 85, 168
S.o. 'Tricolor', 162-3
S. splendens Cleopatra
Series, 16-17
Santolina, 113, 187
S. neapolitana
'Sulphurea', 20-1
sarcococca, 123
Saxifraga, 112, 136
S. longifolia, 159, 187
S. paniculata, 158, 187
Scabiosa, 113, 121, 137, 187
S. atropurpurea
'Cockade', 136

scale insects, 177
scent, 11, 142
crown imperials, 39
evening gardens, 150
semi-shady sites, 115
spring, 28
sunny sites, 107
woodland plants, 86
Schizostylis (Kaffir lily),
113, 137
Scilla (squill), 36, 112, 120,
136, 187
S. siberica (Siberian
squill), 63
Sedum (stonecrop), 107,
113, 137, 187
S. acre, 158
S. anacampseros, 86
S. obtusatum, 134
S. sieboldii 'Medio-
variegatum', 59
S. spathulifolium 'Cape
Blanco', 159
S. spectabile (ice plant),
137
S. spurium 'Tricolor', 158
seeds, sowing, 182
semi-shady sites, 114-21
Sempervivum (houseleek),
61, 85, 112, 137, 187
Senecio, 183, 187
S. x *hybridus* (cineraria),
78-9, 112
S. maritima, 20-1, 27, 113
shady sites, 54-5, 86-7, 122-9
shells, 86-7
shrubs, 11, 132
locations, 110, 123, 126,
134
pruning, 181
supports, 172
Siberian squill *(Scilla
siberica)*, 63
sinks, 85-7, 158-9
Skimmia, 120, 123, 126,
128, 187
S. japonica 'Rubella', 26-7
S. reevesiana, 164
slugs, 176
snails, 176
snake's head fritillary
(Fritillaria meleagris),
86-7, 120, 128, 185
snapdragons *see
Antirrhinum*
soil: acid, 24, 78, 118
hygiene, 176
planting and repotting,
178
Solanum capsicastrum
(winter cherry), 26, 113,
120, 126, 187
Solomon's seal
(Polygonatum x
hybridum), 38, 120,
128, 187
southernwood *(Artemisia)*,
21, 107, 113, 115, 136,
184

spider plants
(Chlorophytum), 126,
184
spruces, 26, 76, 133, 186
spurge *(Euphorbia)*, 101,
112, 113, 136, 185
squills *see Scilla*
stag horn ferns, 123
stakes, 46, 172
standards, 59, 144, 170-1
statice *(Limonium
sinuatum)*, 137
stencilling, 164-5
steps, 142-3
stocks *(Matthiola)*, 8-9, 113
stone containers, 27, 85,
86-7, 158, 178
stonecrop *(Sedum)*, 59, 86,
113, 134, 137, 158-9, 187
strawberries, 46, 83, 113
succulents, 61, 85, 107, 134
sumach *(Rhus)*, 137
sun roses (X *Halimiocistus)*,
64-5
sunny positions, 106-13
supports, 172-3
swan river daisies, 15
sweet peas *(Lathyrus)*, 113
sweet Williams, 177

T

Tagetes (French marigold),
112, 137, 187
T. patula 'Spanish
Brocade', 161
tarragon, 168, 169
Taxus (yew), 110, 123, 126,
166, 187
T. cuspidata, 26
terraces, 116-17
terracotta pots, 9, 124
frost-proof, 26
glazed, 56-7
hygiene, 178
weathering, 31, 38
window boxes, 15, 28-9
Thuja, 139, 187
T. orientalis 'Aurea Nana',
27
Thunbergia alata (black-
eyed Susan), 69, 112,
187
Thymus (thyme), 113, 187
T. drucei, 168
T. vulgaris aureus, 169
tobacco plants *see
Nicotiana*
Tolmiea menziesii (pick-a-
back plant), 51, 61, 115,
121, 126, 129, 187
tomatoes, 83, 113
topiary, 166-7
Tovara virginiana
'Painter's Palette', 51
trachelospermum, 9
Tradescantia (wandering
Jew), 113, 121, 187
T. fluminensis 'Variegata',

16-17, 170, 182, 183
tree ferns, 123, 170
trees, 11
chrysanthemum 'trees', 59
conifers, 76
fruit trees, 107
in roof gardens, 132
shade from, 115
supports, 172
trellises, 172-3
trompe l'oeil, 164
Tropaeolum (nasturtium),
137, 149, 187
T. majus, 113
T.m. 'Alaska', 22-3,
136
troughs, 85, 90-1
Tsuga canadensis, 26
tubs, 74-83
Tulipa (tulips), 10, 34-5,
75, 110, 112, 120, 128,
136, 187
T. 'Ancilla' (waterlily
tulip), 30-1
T. 'Carnival de Nice', 70
T. 'Concerto', 61
T. 'Flaming Parrot', 35
T. 'Garden Party', 137
T. 'Greuze', 72
T. 'Monte Carlo', 102-3
T. 'Peach Blossom', 28-9
T. 'Picture', 35
T. 'Plaisir', 61
T. 'Queen of Night', 75
T. 'Redwing', 35
T. 'Toronto', 61

U

Ulex (gorse), 136
urns, 68-73
uvularia, 86

V

Vaccinium (blueberry), 83,
136
valerian *(Centranthus)*,
137
vegetables, 83
vegetative propagation,
182
x *Venidio-arctotis*, 113,
187
Verbena, 9, 15, 52, 94,
107, 113, 134, 140
V. x *hybrida* 'Showtime',
97, 108
V. x *hybrida* 'Silver
Anne', 45
V. 'Sissinghurst', 112
V. tenera 'Mahonettii', 66
Versailles tubs, 75, 148
Viburnum, 123
V. tinus (laurustinus),
120
Vinca (periwinkle), 120,
128, 187
V. 'La Grave', 72

V. minor (lesser periwinkle), 63
vine barrels, 78-9
Viola (pansies), 6, 20, 38-9, 61, 66, 85, 96, 113, 115, 116, 120, 121, 123, 128, 129, 131, 136, 181, 187
V. 'Rhine Gold', 96
V. x *wittrockiana*, 116, 121
V. x *w.* Universal Series, 38-9
violets, dog's tooth (*Erythronium* 'Pagoda'), 86-7

W

wall baskets, 93, 98-9
wallflowers (*Cheiranthus*), 112, 116, 136
walls, 146
wandering Jew (*Tradescantia*), 16-17, 113, 121, 170, 182-3, 187
water gardens, 75, 110
water hyacinth (*Eichhornia acicularis*), 110
water lettuce (*Pistia stratiotes*), 110
water lilies (*Nymphaea*), 75, 110, 113, 186

watering, 139, 180
in exposed sites, 132-3
hanging baskets, 180
herb towers, 169
spraying, 24
sunny sites, 107
window boxes, 15
weathering containers, 9, 31, 38
Weigela, 112, 187
W. 'Looymansii Aurea', 72-3
whiteflies, 177
wind, exposed sites, 131
windflowers (*Anemone*), 101, 112, 120, 184

window boxes, 14-31
decorating wooden, 164-5
planting, 16
wooden, 15, 162-3
winter aconite (*Eranthis hyemalis*), 113
winter cherry (*Solanum capsicastrum*), 26, 113, 120, 126, 187
wood: troughs, 85, 90-1
window boxes, 15, 162-5
woodland gardens, 86-7
woodlice, 176
woodwardias, 123

Y

yew (*Taxus*), 26, 110, 123, 126, 166, 187
Yucca, 107, 113, 121, 137, 187
Y. gloriosa, 116-17

Z

Zantedeschia hybrid (arum lily), 121
Zinnia, 107, 187
Z. elegans, 18-19, 112-13

ACKNOWLEDGMENTS

The author would like to thank the following people for their help on *Container Gardening*: Charlotte Fraser, whose horticultural help throughout the book was invaluable; Jenny and Richard Raworth, Mrs. P. Franklin and Sarah Franklin, Anne Mollo, Kathleen Darby, Mr and Mrs D. Zelouf, and Mrs. B. Hervey for allowing us to photograph in their gardens; Ken Vincent of Terracotta UK of Covent Garden, who was so generous in supplying many containers; Sally Tamplin for the loan of her beautiful wire plant stand; The Garden History Museum and The Chelsea Physic Garden for the loan of their old garden tools; and Brinkman Brothers for supplying trees.

Also Quentin Roake for all his support and assistance; and especially Stephen Bennington, May Cristea, Veronica Hitchcock, Alex Starkey, and Roddy Wood; Sally Smallwood, who art directed the book until the arrival of baby Joe; and Project Editor, Mary-Clare Jerram, and Art Editor, Kevin Ryan, for being such an understanding team.

Dorling Kindersley would like to thank Hilary Bird for compiling the index; Richard Bird, Damien Moore, and Gillian Prince for editorial help; Steve Cluett and Kevin Williams for design help; and Steve Dobson and Greg Matanle for assisting Matthew Ward with photography at Plough Studios.

All photographs by Matthew Ward, except: A.G.E. Fotostock 7; L'Ami des Jardins/J.F. Jarreau *169*; Boys Syndication/Jacqui Hurst *33, 92, 107, 123, 135, 144* (bottom); Eric Crichton *85, 87* (top); *93*; Geoff Dann *22-3, 24-5*; English Flower Garden/John Murray *6*; Fisons plc *176, 177*; Garden Picture Library/ Brian Carter *69, 74, 118*; Garden Picture Library/Derek Fell *110* (top); Garden Picture Library/John Neubauer *130*; Garden Picture Library/Ron Sutherland *11, 106, 149* (bottom), *166*; Garden Picture Library/Steve Wooster *143*; Derek Harris *9, 10* (top and bottom), *140*; Jacqui Hurst *61, 84, 124-5, 127, 131, 132-3, 148, 150,151*;

ICI Agrochemicals *176, 177*; Insight/Linda Burgess *8, 14, 32, 134, 142, 146-7*; Graham Kirk *50, 67* (top), *164-5, 166*; Steve Robson *139, 149* (top); Shell U.K. *176*; Harry Smith *76, 177*; Michael Warren *177*; and Steve Wooster *115*.

SPECIALIST SUPPLIERS

~ CONTAINERS ~

DOBIES GARDEN CENTRES,
Lasswade, Midlothian, Scotland EH18 1AZ

KARIN HESSENBERG,
235 Upland Road, London SE22 0DJ
Handmade pottery

JANE NORBURY,
Unit 7, 36-38 Peckham Road,
London SE5 7OI
Handmade pottery

SOUTHSIDE GARDEN CENTRE,
Kilternan, County Dublin, Eire

TERRACOTTA UK,
New Covent Garden Market, Nine Elms,
London SW8 5NH

~ PLANTS ~

GREEN FARM PLANTS,
Bentley, Farnham, Surrey GU10 5JX

REGINALD KAYE LTD,
Waithman Nurseries, Silverdale, Carnforth,
Lancashire LA5 0TY
Ferns, alpines, perennials

PERRYHILL NURSERIES,
Hartfield, Sussex TN7 4JP
Shrubs, roses, perennials

~ CONTAINERS AND PLANTS ~

CLIFTON NURSERIES LTD,
Clifton Villas, Warwick Avenue,
London W9 2PH

WISLEY PLANT CENTRE,
RHS Garden, Near Ripley, Woking,
Surrey GU23 6QB